Design City
Tokyo

This publication is designed to provide accurate and authoritative information in regard to the subject matter covered. It is sold on the understanding
that the Publisher is not engaged in rendering professional services. If professional advice or other expert assistance is required, the services of a
competent professional should be sought.

Other Wiley Editorial Offices

John Wiley & Sons Inc., 111 River Street, Hoboken, NJ 07030, USA

Jossey-Bass, 989 Market Street, San Francisco, CA 94103-1741, USA

Wiley-VCH Verlag GmbH, Boschstr. 12, D-69469 Weinheim, Germany

John Wiley & Sons Australia Ltd, 33 Park Road, Milton, Queensland 4064,
Australia

John Wiley & Sons (Asia) Pte Ltd, 2 Clementi Loop #02-01, Jin Xing
Distripark, Singapore 129809

John Wiley & Sons Canada Ltd, 22 Worcester Road, Etobicoke, Ontario,
Canada M9W 1L1

ISBN 0470093641

Printed and bound by Conti Tipocolor, Italy

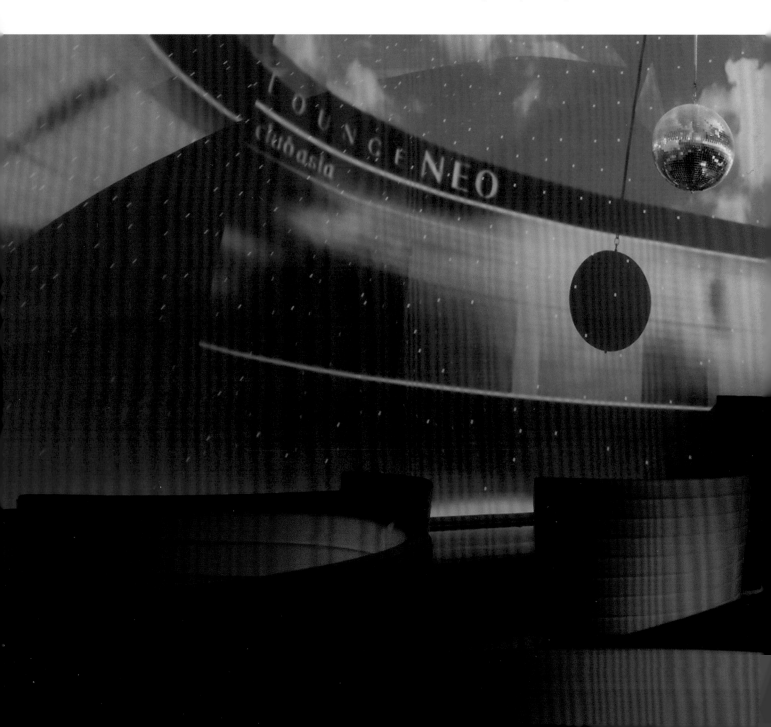

Design City
Tokyo

Masaaki Takahashi

Series Designer **Liz Sephton**

contents

Acknowledgements

I would like to show my appreciation to all those at Wiley-Academy who helped me develop and realise this project. Especially, I would like to thank Helen Castle, who I have got to know since contributing to *Architectural Design* and who has given me this opportunity to publish this project. I also appreciate all the editorial support of Mariangela Palazzi-Williams and Famida Rasheed, as well as of the copy-editor Lucy Isenberg. I would also like to thank those at the Brizhead office in Tokyo: for the editorial assistance of Yumi Kuramoto and Charles J Ayres. I greatly appreciate the advice of Tsunehiko Yoshida on Japanese interior design history; Makoto Oikawa for suggesting all the new industry information; and Hiroyuki Hattori for giving me hints about the various areas of Tokyo. I also give my sincerest thanks and respect to the many photographers, designers and industry insiders who helped make this book a reality.

Photo credits

pp 1, 4(t), 16–17, 52–9 photos: © Nacasa & Partners ®; pp 2–3, 190–2, 193(tl+bl), 194–5 photos: © Nacasa & Partners ®; pp 4(b), 13, 63, 90–5, 106–110, 111(b), 112–13, 124–9 photos: © Kozo Takayama; pp 5(tr), 15(l), 102–3, 130–4, 135(tl+ml+bl), 210–13, 214(t), 214–5 photos: © Daici Ano; pp 5(b), 183, 196–8, 199(tl+bl), 200–3 photos: © Cube Communications Co. Ltd; pp 5(tl), 139, 168–71, 172(t), 173 photos: © Makota Yoshida; pp 7, 12(b), 14, 15(r), 25(t), 216–17 photos: © Mario Bettella; pp 8, 9, 10, 11 photos: © Masahiro Ishibashi; p 12(t) photos: © Takeshi Taira; pp 19–24, photos: © Ken Suzuki; pp 26–8, 29(tl+tr) photos: © Masahiro Ishibashi; p 29(b); pp 30–5 photos: © Yoshio Shiratori; pp 36–41, 70–75, 156–60, 161(tr+br) photos: © Nacasa & Partners ®; pp 42–5 photos: © Nacasa & Partners; pp 46–51 photos © Kenichi Suzuki, en-ma co Ltd; pp 60–1, 76–81, 140–2, 143(tl+tr) photos: © Daici Ano; pp 64–9, 96–101 photos: © Hikaru Suzuki; pp 82–9 photos: © Seishi Maeda; pp 104–5, 114–18, 119(t) photos: © Toshihisa Ishii; pp 120–3 photos: © Masayuki Hayashi; pp 136–7, 144(t), 145–9, 184–6, 187(t), 188–9 Mitsumasa Fujitsuka; pp 150–3, 154(t), 155 photos: © Nobuyosi Meguro; p 162 photos: © Marie Watanebe; pp 163–5, 166(t), 167 photos: © Shinichi Ogawa & Associates; pp 174–6, 177(l+tr), 178–9 photos: © Naoya Kawabe; pp 204–6, 207 (t+br), 208–9 photos: © Nacasa & Partners ®;

A History of Modern Japanese Interiors in Tokyo

In modern-day Japan many foreign designers and architects actively contribute to the ever-changing cityscape. Unlike the designers who floated in on the Bubble Economy's wave of capital in the 1980s, they came of their own accord and have made Tokyo their base. By comparison with Western cities that have relatively strict building codes, Tokyo has the immense appeal that, aside from regulations governing fire prevention and earthquake precautions, designers often have free rein to realise virtually any type of design. Furthermore, although a vast city, Tokyo retains many districts that seem more like individual villages and so act as further stimuli to the designer's imagination.

Introduction

Below immense modern buildings lurk wood plank houses and wooden apartments that appear flimsy enough to leak when it rains. These dwellings sit in the depths of labyrinthine streets where the residents carry on a traditional lifestyle. Billboards and banners flood the streets and TV monitors light up not only the shopping and entertainment districts but the insides of trains as well. Shops and restaurants make use of a whole bag of design tricks, and the shops in the chic areas might as well be chanting the mantra 'design or die'.

Previously, they went about their business with the slogan, 'Catch up and overtake the West', but at some point along the way this catchphrase seemed to disappear. The world of design exhibits the same trend. The designers of yesteryear used to yearn to be in London, Milan or New York. However, with the passage of time the Japanese began to appreciate that at home around them they had an architecture and interior design scene that surpassed the West.

Above: Dior Omotesando, 2003.
In keeping with Dior's reputation for unparalleled elegance, this high-profile location along one of Tokyo's most fashionable shopping boulevards has inspired designers Kazuyo Sejima + Ryue Nishizawa/SANAA. By night passers-by are drawn to the subtly lit windows, their draped acrylic screens replacing the ubiquitous fabric variety

Below: Comme des Garçons Aoyama, 1999.
As befits a piece of design with an eye on the new millennium, designers Future Systems have created a truly arresting showcase for this iconic fashion label fashion – a cutting-edge design for a sophisticated market in a sophisticated location

In the early 1960s, Tokyo's architectural design machine switched into action with the announcement that the city had been selected to host the 1964 Olympic Games, an opportunity that stimulated Tokyo's evolution into a modern world city and fuelled urban regeneration. Some parts of Tokyo still resembled a burnt wasteland, the result of aerial bombardment towards the end of the Second World War when the Allied Forces indiscriminately bombed both industrial and residential areas.

For the most part, the Japanese were enthused by this surge of development, and the value of design became more widely appreciated. Another important influence was the big changes sweeping the fashion industry in the 1960s. Trendsetting fashion retailers shifted from the confines of the department store to include the clothing manufacturers. The brand leaders forged the way ahead with their innovative presentation of men's and women's clothing. Companies such as Kanebo and Renown planned and developed their merchandise in tandem with the department stores. Fashion started to affect the look of interior retail space and the design of the stores became much more sophisticated, Shinjuku Tokano being a well-known example. Whereas previously the design divisions of building contractors had created most of the interiors for stores and commercial facilities, designers now broke away to become independent businesses in their own right. Interior design emerged as a separate profession.

Shiro Kuramata

Shiro Kuramata (1934–91), who founded his office in 1965 in Tokyo, was a great designer who had a tremendous impact on the development of Japanese contemporary design. Having previously worked for the design division of department stores and fashion designers, one of Kuramata's greatest achievements was the way he incorporated art into interior design. The mid-20th

Above: **Flower base #2, 1989**.
Shiro Kuramata is renowned for incorporating art and sculpture into his interior design. This small acrylic vase is an elegant example of his sensitivity to urban form

Below: **Laputa, 1991**.
Perched on the 26th floor of a building on the waterfront of Tokyo's Ten'nozu Isle, an area accessed via the Tokyo Monorail running out of Hamamatsucho, the sushi bar offers stunning views out over the harbour and cityscape while inside the eye is treated to Kuramata's unrivalled and quintessentially Japanese elegance

century international art scene had shifted its nucleus from Paris to New York with the spawning of Abstract Expressionism and then Minimalism. The Minimalist artist Donald Judd (1928–94) inspired Kuramata with his three-dimensional sculptures that expressed a deep regard for the city. Indeed, some of Kuramata's furniture bears a direct resemblance to Judd's work. Kuramata had a taste for using materials and metals with a transparent quality such as acrylic and aluminium, the novelty of which appealed to people. His interest in these materials originated with his experience of seeing American bombers drop sparkling aluminium strips to cloud enemy radarscopes during the war. Kuramata created many works that emphasise a sense of floating and seem liberated from the forces of gravity. He worked single-mindedly, intent on bestowing a dream world on those who used his creations. He spoke of aesthetics in very Japanese terms saying, 'The appeal of commercial design is its ephemeral nature, its potential to be extinguished and its experimental aspects. In other words it is like a play with intermissions.' Just as he had envisioned, over time even most of his own pieces went out of production, and only very recently have people started to reproduce them. Of his interior projects, not more than a dozen remain, among them a sushi bar named Laputa, in eastern Shinagawa, designed in 1991. However, his influence still carries weight in today's world, and many designers still worship him.

The 1970s

Kuramata and his peers, with their memories dating back to prewar Japan, were the first to be initiated into postwar American design and culture. The 1970 Osaka Exposition, however, heralded the second generation of postwar designers who made their appearance in the 1970s. Although the exposition was held in Osaka rather than Tokyo, it stimulated Japanese design culture in a similar manner to the Olympics in the early 1960s. Two designers representative

Below: **Laputa, 1991.** The upper portion of the large translucent partition has holes to hold flowers

of this generation are Shigeru Uchida (1943–) who opened his shop in 1970, and Takashi Sugimoto (1945–), who established his Super Potato office in 1971. Their output exemplifies this period's shop and restaurant designs and they are still active today. Many of their apprentices went on to become excellent designers in their own right.

The emergence of the young as the key players in fashion stands out as a characteristic of the 1970s fashion world. This trend has persisted so that today young people continue to break down the pre-existing notions of fashion, art and design. From this era young people's fervour for fashion grew and the jobs of interior designers expanded as well. Fashion and interiors have a symbiotic relationship; both draw inspiration from one another, and the boutiques of this era began to showcase the cutting edge of interior design. It was in 1973 that Rei Kawakubo (1942–) established Comme des Garçons, and afterwards Japanese fashion designers began to be acclaimed for their international collections.

At the time, both Yohji Yamamoto (1943–) and Rei Kawakubo worked on projects that had the common theme of 'fake poverty'. They took raw fabric and made it wrinkled, and also altered fabrics to make their edges look as if insects had eaten into them. They used uneven dye techniques to make their materials look washed out and tore holes in fabrics in order to give the clothes a used look. Yamamoto and Kawakubo both have a monastic or Zen-like outlook and often use monochromatic and black-based colour schemes while cutting the clothes to obscure the wearer's body-shape. In 1982, both designers showed prêt-à-porter collections in Paris, but they had already been attracting worldwide attention since the late 1970s. The influence of the 'Eastern Shock' rippled throughout the European fashion world and also garnered domestic interest in Japan where it attracted many followers. Recently, the Japanese clothing market has matured. Possibly some in the Japanese industry had anticipated this and

Above: Prada Aoyama, 2003.
The building's glass blocks reflect their surroundings in a novel integration with the cityscape. Around the building's perimeter are mossy banks that conceal storage areas. So architecturally innovative is the project that impressed visitors can buy a photobook describing it

Left: Prada Aoyama, 2003.
To reverse the recession that hit Japan in the 1990s, in 2002 legislation was enacted to boost the real estate market. With construction attractive again, famous foreign designers like Herzog & de Meuron came to work in Tokyo. Their arresting design for this Prada store sees the building rise from the second-floor basement to the above-ground seventh floor. The interior's perpendicular core supports the floors to avoid overloading the glass blocks that create the building's skin. Inside, the fitting rooms seem like horizontal tubes inserted between floors

indeed had been preparing themselves for it since the late 1970s. Heightened consumer awareness and the positive economic climate helped conceive the 1980s fervour for fashion. This in turn made waves in the world of design.

The 1980s

The 1980s saw young people's interest in fashion peak. The styles in evidence in London in the late 1970s and even after the 1980s saw a very strong link between music and fashion. However, this connection did not hold as much sway in Japan where the numbers influenced by music were relatively small. Fashion became a mass phenomenon, which exploded with unprecedented force. For example, in a single year the design company Plastic Studio took on responsibility for fitting out between 150 and 200 boutiques – though most of them were franchises or shops within shops. It was at this time that the DC and Designers and Characters labels (the former operating internationally, the latter being the domestic brand) became buzzwords, and the young sank much of their income into buying clothes. When boutiques announced sales, queues of young people would form, snaking around the outside of stores. However, from the late 1980s fashion trends gradually moved towards more casual looks

Below: One Omotesando, 2003.
On a thoroughfare in one of Tokyo's prime shopping locations Kenzo Kuma Four have designed an imposing emporium that accommodates some of fashion's most powerful names. Inside a building whose granular Japanese larchwood louvres give an elegant nod to the surrounding culture, international brands like the LVMH (Moët Hennessy-Louis Vuitton) Group, Fendi, Celine, Loewe and Donna Karan stake their ground

and the brands that are now internationally renowned came to the fore. Fashion's influence extended beyond the bounds of clothing and began to affect the look of eating and drinking establishments, as people became far more design conscious. Whereas the 1960s and 1970s saw little attention to, or investment in, the design of restaurants and bars, by the 1980s this had completely changed. People began to give themselves job titles such as 'space designer' or 'space producer'. The media also began to give coverage to the clubs and café bars (dining bars) these people designed. This led to a café-bar boom.

The famous Nishi-Azabu establishment, Red Shoes, is said to have started this trend, becoming a hang-out for designers, musicians and artists. Around this time people began to consider interior design a glamorous profession (in 2003, Red Shoes was resurrected, this time in southern Aoyama). The 1980s café-bar boom soon fizzled out, but it served as the precursor to the designer-restaurant boom of the 1990s. The expanding Bubble Economy of the 1980s set the scene for these developments and market conditions profoundly influenced the values of the Japanese.

In part, Tokyo's rising land values and real estate prices prompted unparalleled economic prosperity in the 1980s which led to excessive levels of cash in circulation. People lavished large sums on dwellings and interiors, many of which were of dubious quality given the amount of money expended on them. Some clients even had traders go to the trouble of importing Italian marble by airfreight. Designers such as Mario Bellini, Mario Botta, Nigel Coates, Peter Eisenman, Michael Graves, Jean Graves, Jean Nouvel, Richard Rogers, Philippe Starck and Rafael Viñoly were all called in from abroad and worked without constraints on their creativity. Zaha Hadid planned on doing her first architecture project in Tokyo, though the scheme was eventually abandoned. Of course, Japanese architects also had many opportunities to realise their own creations. The national and Tokyo municipal governments sank vast sums into large-scale, unrealistically ambitious and eventually money-losing projects, and put forward numerous plans for redevelopment centred around the Tokyo Bay area. While some of these reached completion, many were never built.

The 1990s and beyond

With the Plaza Accord of 1985, the Japanese government entered the foreign exchange market and the rising yen was tied into the world economy. From the late 1980s land prices increased dramatically and many people, especially businessmen, began to bemoan the high cost of buying houses in Japan's cities. The high price of property became a national problem and in 1990, in order to combat it, property standardisation laws were enacted that, among other things, introduced a property tax. The Ministry of Finance fast-tracked regulations governing real estate investment and the flow of capital from financial institutions into real estate came to a halt. By mobilising the tax system and curtailing finances they tried to depress land values, and the subsequent dramatic reduction in real estate prices caused the Japanese property market to collapse. As Japanese real estate prices fell, investment in real estate ceased. This is how the Bubble Economy burst in 1991; the aftermath has seen a long and severe recession wrack Japan. Yet despite this there was a boom in the mid-1990s in eating out. The restaurant industry was where the most talented designers started to converge. 'Designer restaurant' became a new category whereby the customers' interests widened beyond cooking and management and extended to interior design. The designers who were active from this period might be identified as the third postwar generation. A few high-profile designers raked in the business while the majority took on low-cost projects. Also, stores and commercial facilities were endlessly being built only to be scrapped and taken down. In order to construct something one needs sufficient faith in the architectural project to gather people and money together. This is true in any city,

Above: **Hakka, 2003.**
Tokyo is a high-density city. In this design Yasuhiro Yamashita and his atelier Tekut solve the problem of constraints on space with a novel three-storey steel structure on a site area of 57.16 square metres. Though small, the house can accommodate a three-person family within a simple construction with little interior partitioning

Below: **Coredo Nihonbashi, 2004.**
The new millennium has seen a boom in Tokyo's commercial and office construction. A prime example is this cutting-edge complex designed by Kohn Pedersen Fox Associates, a 20-storey flagship building that boasts international accountancy firm Merrill Lynch as its main tenant

Above: Undercover Lab, 2001.
In an extraordinary adaptation of programme to place, this landmark building houses a studio, press showroom and office within its startling form. Set back 10 metres from the road, it features a section that extends out like a tube

but especially true in Tokyo. From 2002, despite the recession, the government revitalised the residential market, luring people back into real estate by such measures as lowering interest rates on home loans. This led to what people termed a 'mini-bubble'. Major construction companies and firms now build many hotels, offices, high-rise apartment buildings and commercial facilities without fear of glutting the market. Caretta Shiodome and Roppongi Hills are recent examples of such developments. These projects have a fairly high regard for design compared with previous schemes and use many famous foreign architects. Herzog & de Meuron's Prada store and Massimiliano Fuksas' Emporio Armani are the most conspicuous exponents of this trend for using foreign designers and these stores have enjoyed international press coverage. That confidence in the Japanese economy has been regained is manifested by international fashion brands such as Prada and Louis Vuitton investing in large-scale stores.

Japan has a relatively high rate of economic dependence on the construction industry. With little flat land and roughly the same surface area as California, Japan has six million construction-industry workers, outnumbering the US total by about 30 per cent. Including repair and maintenance costs, the investment in construction for Western countries rests at around 10 per cent of the total GDP while in Japan it reaches 20 per cent. Exactly how these jobs exist in this small country remains a puzzle. The clichéd term 'designer' has come to apply to dwellings, and estate agents now sell 'designer residences' and 'designer apartments'. Recent apartment advertising stresses lifestyle image over simply the architecture, often emphasising the surrounding landscape and nightscape, as well as featuring attractive male and female models. Codan (the Urban Development Corporation), which previously led Japan's compound housing projects, has utilised the talents of popular architects to build large-scale architectural projects such as the Shinnonome Canal Cort Codan by Toyoo Ito and Kengo Kuma. Though this move largely changed the image of Codan, in reality, whether houses or compound dwellings, it is still work in progress. At the same time, a class of mainly young people has started to commission architects, rather than local engineers or carpenters, to construct their dwellings. One should take note of the customers' ability to refuse colour-by-numbers design as clients now get custom-made exteriors, interiors and layout with an individualised design.

Today the Japanese design consciousness that went from clothes to food establishments to dwellings has expanded to unprecedented levels. The rationality of the West coexists with the chaos of the East. The style of Japan that embraces this disorder will continue to evolve and its transformation will probably never stop. Japanese designers, even if facing constraints of budget and space, continue to make efforts to improve their ideas while seeking to revolutionise design and creativity. The chaos and imbalance strengthen the energies of creation. As the heart of the movement in Japanese design, Tokyo areas such as Roppongi, Nishi Azabu and Daikanyama will continue to spawn new trends.

In today's world of fashion it has become difficult to create something completely new as designers seem to do little more than rehash the styles of the past. Apparel is said to be the smallest form of architecture and it seems that, equally, in terms of built architecture the innovation of the present age has stagnated. Recently, architects have taken a fancy to neat designs that incorporate multiple uses of glass. Its transparency evokes lightness and expansiveness, and its use is a trend that has spread across many cities, including Tokyo. Many similar-looking shopping complexes have been built. As a result, it would seem the expression of design has become more homogenised and the once strong sense of individuality or uniqueness has been lost. Rather than giving just adequate consideration to adapt to the context, there is too much adaptation and buildings get lost in the context which results in the loss of a sense of presence. Ultimately the trend towards translucency also seems to link to the capacity to erase one's own existence. It would appear that the grammar of architectural language has been exhausted. However, while architecture seems to have become homogenised, interior design shows that designers still have the power to create a diversity of things that coexist with strong individuality in design. As a city, Tokyo does not hesitate to express desire and maintains a very open feeling towards it. In every corner of the city one sees 'expressed desire', something which extends even into the homes of individuals. Japanese cities have little self-control in terms of maintaining order, which allows design not only to encapsulate desire but to express it. It is manifested in symbols and messages (capitalism's trademark logos and brand advertising) and is expressed in the form of architectural space with design that can serve any purpose. Those who send these visual messages (mostly companies) want

Above: Motoazabu Hills, 2002.
Set in an old neighbourhood and surrounded by traditional houses and temples, this 29-storey, 100-meter-high residential complex was designed by Shojo Uchii – a modern yet visually comfortable solution to Tokyo's problem of scarce housing

to showcase their products and get people to buy. As a result, everything from giant billboards to cases displaying cleverly crafted wax samples of food turn the streets of the city into visual arteries conveying advertising messages to consumers. For their part, consumers scan the city's plethora of symbols and messages for products that will fulfil their desires. Both producers and consumers stay faithful to their desires as design becomes the medium of their communication. In Tokyo, this evolved form of communication is highly visible.

People's needs and desires in terms of design are powerful and because of this there is fierce competition between designers. People crave designs they won't tire of: spaces to savour delicious food, spaces to display merchandise beautifully, as well as spaces that let them live the lifestyle they want. Capital becomes concentrated in order to meet – or possibly create – this demand. Clients support the designers and this process will continue into the future. In this process, or movement, design becomes a method as well as a purpose, form as well as content, and people consciously as well as subconsciously comprehend this.

Above: SONY Building, 1966.
The bustling centre of Ginza, with its busy subway and streets filled with traffic, sports some of Tokyo's largest commercial buildings. Here the streamlined exterior of the SONY Building, with Hermès to the left, dwarfs the streetlife below

Right: Maison Hermès Tokyo, 2001.
On top of the building a statue of a horse and the banners of this international brand survey the crowds far below. Hermès' imposing outpost in Tokyo lends conviction to the continued high profile of Japan as a design-market mover and shaker

From the high-powered owners of top-end designer restaurant chains to the immensely popular ramen noodle sales operations with an annual turnover worth $760 million, Tokyo hosts a great variety of cooking and business styles. Many Japanese entrepreneurs are happy to sink their venture capital not into Web companies or high-tech schemes but rather into the incredibly dynamic bar and restaurant sector. The industry generated by eating out creates the gold mines of Tokyo; the money pouring into it is on a par with investment in the automobile industry. In recent years things have become more radical as negative growth drives up competition, and so store design is often an integral part of business strategy. Recently, popular eating and drinking establishments have come to integrate the following three attributes: a shift towards 'wafu', darkness and individual rooms.

The first facet, wafu, is more or less synonymous with Japanese style but one must use such terms carefully as their nuances and the things they refer to differ. Wafu doesn't include purely Japanese architecture and Japanese styles, nor does it refer to styles from ancient times. Wafu is a term that became current relatively recently, after Western architecture had permeated Japanese culture. When Japanese compared domestic styles to Western architecture they created the word to reinterpret the essence of Japanese architecture in Western architectural language. One can see a specific example in many private dwellings incorporating tea-ceremony styles based on the Minimalism of sukiya-zukuri that now incorporate modern materials such as plastic and metal. Non-Japanese can probably build in a proto-Japanese style, but only designers well versed in Japanese culture can comprehend wafu. Also, since Japanese design fundamentally makes use of the widest possible range of materials and is a thing of simple construction, wafu can easily absorb foreign architectural styles and elements to give birth to something new. Interestingly, everything that has been said so far would fit Japanese cuisine as well. As a result of the fear of BSE (mad cow disease) many restaurants now shun cooking with meat. The demand for Japanese cuisine has grown correspondingly, and obviously the mainstream of the design world tends to lean towards Japanese styling.

Eat

Although the next attribute is darkness, the Japanese usually keep things bright both inside and out with fluorescent lights. Restaurants use lighting other than fluorescent lighting as well as indirect illumination to produce a relaxed atmosphere. Particularly in the past few years they use especially dim lighting, perhaps a reflection of the psychological state of their patrons. During the continuing recession it is possible that people seek out darker spaces in order to escape reality. The penchant for dim lighting also relates to the late-1990s pleasure in nightscapes. So important do people consider the nightscape element in restaurants, bars, hotels and housing complexes that

Right: **Soho's Omotesando**. The wine cellar has quite a presence in Soho's Omotesando. A DJ booth has been fitted above it

specialist consultants are now brought in to advise on it. The third attribute, the inclusion of individual rooms, is connected to the trend in darkness. In order for customers to escape life's harsh realities and to promote intimacy with their dining companions, the physical distance between them must be diminished. Consequently, restaurants that offer individual rooms as part of their business cater for the modern desire for individual privacy and seclusion or to the presiding spirit of a younger generation dependent on cell phones for communication. Despite these psychological phenomena the popularity of individual rooms has recently experienced something of a decline.

Soho's Omotesando

Location: Jingumae 6–31–17, Shibuya-ku
Completion Date: 2002

Yuji Hirata (Nomurakougeisha)

V28, an impressively shaped building, is located at one of the epicentres of Tokyo fashion: Harajuku's Omotesando Street, haunt of the well-heeled and fashion-conscious. The building attracts little attention during the daytime but after dark it stands out strikingly like a giant lantern, in colourful patterns of red, blue and purple, with the aid of its shining LED interior lighting curtain-wall. This project heralds the first step in a long-term advance into Japan for the Hong Kong and UK-based developer Veloqx City Investment Ltd. Designed by CDI Aoyama Studio, which is led by British designer Benjamin Warner, the building is conveniently situated directly above a subway station. Zara, an international brand that might be called the Spanish Gap, occupies the first and second floors. At first glance it might be mistaken for another brand-name boutique since many brand-name stores line Omotesando.

In a complex that also house a fitness club and several restaurants, young, fashionable, female shoppers and T-shirt-wearing superfit guys from the gym direct you on your way, while a see-through elevator whisks you up to Soho's on

Above: Soho's Omotesando. The bar counter as seen from the entrance. The luminescent wall aims to appeal to the outside world

Left: Soho's Omotesando. The bold and massive wall is quite light as it is assembled from wood

Above: **Soho's Omotesando**. The exquisite nightscape facing Shinjuku

the fourth and top floor of the building. The restaurant has terrace seating on the roof and people often book it for wedding parties. Unfortunately, the seating is closed off in winter. After passing through an entrance bathed in yellow light, you come out into a spacious area that seats 200 people. At the owner's request, the above-grade ceiling reaches quite high (7.5 metres), a rarity in Japan. However, the roominess proved a challenge for Japanese designers accustomed to designing narrow spaces. The building is itself extremely individualistic and conveying to the outside world that inside lies a restaurant of this scale and substance became a major undertaking. Since the roofs of Harajuku's shops form a row and the street is lined with trees, people's field of vision usually doesn't reach beyond the first floor. Unless the building was viewed from the pavement on the opposite side of the street, it would be difficult to appreciate it in its entirety. The outer wall that sparkles so attractively at night presents only a greyish face during the afternoon, and it didn't attract much attention as only the glass-walled shop on the first floor was clearly visible. After much effort the designers came up with a device to capture that attention. On the window side of the restaurant they built a large wall, which prompts those outside to wonder what the massive wall behind the window is. Since the floor could only stand the same weight as an office, they also had to overcome the construction problem of making the entire interior as light as possible. Consequently the heavy-looking wall is, of course, not solid, but is assembled from pieces of wood. Since the wall tilts inwards, the window-side bar seats have an oppressive air. In contrast, the interior hall feels liberating. A couple of sliding walls cover the kitchen, an ingenious device that allows the restaurant to show it to the customers. The window side has a 9-metre lacquered counter. Seated on the original, graceful, steel highchairs one can sip cocktails while savouring the fantastic night view of Tokyo. The menu features Italian-based international cuisine and is run by Soho's Hospitality, the company that also runs Seiryumon, a restaurant featured later in this section. Soho's also runs two other establishments in Tokyo: Soho's West in Setagaya and Soho's Vino Rosso at Shibuya.

Left: **Soho's Omotesando**. The restaurant feels spacious during the daytime

Left: **Soho's Omotesando**. The metallic counter and original, steel highchairs

Left: **Soho's Omotesando**. Red cloth covers the small party rooms

Right: **Soho's Omotesando**. The bar area, seen from the kitchen side

Left: **Soho's Omotesando**. The wall openings, which usually stay closed, reveal the glass-encased kitchen

Above: **Soho's Omotesando**. Exterior view of the building at night

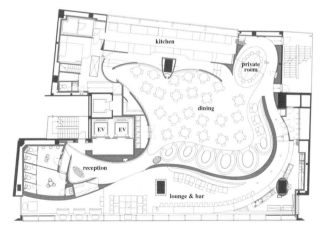

Above: **Soho's Omotesando**. Floor plan

Hoya Hoya

Location: Ebisu-nishi 1–8–3, Shibuya-ku
Completion Date: July 2003

Yusaku Kaneshiro

When you go in through the glazed entrance, the extraordinary interior of this establishment leaves you momentarily speechless. Large flower buds made out of transparent glass and steel tinted green, blue and yellow burst forth throughout the premises. In between these buds sit decorations that bring to mind plants or smaller buds which emit light. These cover most of the walls, ceilings and other surfaces, while below flowing water burbles between stones. The restaurant feels as though it has no empty space; it is a dense jungle of glass. Booths for couples and small groups can be seen within the giant buds.

In the past few years Tokyo's restaurant business has seen a boom in individual rooms to accommodate small parties. Resembling cocoons or earthen huts, for a while they created quite a stir, but recently restaurants have come to offer individual rooms that are not completely covered and shielded from view. This deft move strikes a chord with modern commercial culture's contradictory psychology of wanting to hide from people's view while at the same time wanting to be seen.

Those who can only equate Japanese design with Minimalism are certainly in for a shock. The visitor to Japan can also experience places with excessive design that enjoy their share of popularity. Japanese architecture is not merely about the simple and the concise. Places such as western Kyoto's Katsura Detached Palace, famous for its exquisite buildings and beautifully laid-out gardens and walkways, stand in polar opposition to such Minimalism. There can be found Nikko Toshogu, a mausoleum and resting place for the first of the Edo shoguns, Ieyasu Tokugawa. The Nikko Toshogu is considerably more popular with tourists

Above: Hoya Hoya. As if in a jungle, plant-like decorations are everywhere

Left: Hoya Hoya. The counter seats on the glass floor look as though they are floating

Above: **Hoya Hoya**. The small, bud-like party rooms are encased in glass so there is no feeling of claustrophobia

than with the Japanese. A fabulous and flamboyant building, it realises a Baroque passion not highly esteemed by architects.

One reason for Hoya Hoya's break from traditional Japanese Minimalism is the fact that the restaurant's designer, Kaneshiro, hails from Okinawa, an island between Japan and China that has continued to be influenced by both countries. It had its own independent dynasty and flourishing culture, but after the Second World War it was occupied by American troops whose presence profoundly influenced the indigenous culture. Hence Kaneshiro has been familiar with hybrid culture since childhood. In Japan's interior design world, with its tendency to become homogenised, designers such as Kaneshiro who possess their own strong and distinctive sense of style stand out. His taste and style display a Japanese sensibility towards beauty while possessing elements stylistically in line with Antonio Gaudí. While he may appear the archetypal artisan, in reality Kaneshiro possesses a keen business acumen. He prioritises achieving increased turnover for a restaurant and advises on menus and management. Hoya Hoya serves Japanese food and its spare ribs and soba noodles are very popular. It is designed to complement the state of its food – fresh, soft and warm.

Kaneshiro makes a habit of jotting down the details of things he sees in his dreams, and one night he dreamt he was drinking alcohol while enveloped in sensuous flower buds. This became the concept for the restaurant. His dream garden that became a reality is situated in the basement of a building on the west side of Ebisu station, in a small street clustered with bars and restaurants.

Above: **Hoya Hoya**. Flower-bud seating near the entrance

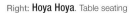

Right: **Hoya Hoya**. Table seating

Above left: Hoya Hoya. A divided mirror on the mezzanine ceiling makes the area look more spacious

Above right: Hoya Hoya. This showcases modern Baroque, Tokyo style

Above: Hoya Hoya. Wooden tables on the mezzanine

Above: **Hoya Hoya**. Sand beneath the reinforced glass floor evokes a Kyoto rock garden's water

Above: **Hoya Hoya**. Computer-generated image of the interior

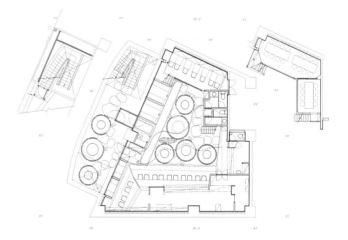

Above: **Hoya Hoya**. Floorplan

Renma Shibuya

Location: Udagawa-cho 24–2, Shibuya-ku
Completion Date: 2003

Noriyoshi Muramatsu

The infamous Scramble Square intersection in Shibuya overflows with people waiting for the lights to change. Once they change to green, people rush out in all directions and miraculously they do not often crash into each other. The front of Shibuya station is the point of origin for Tokyo's youth culture. The name 'Shibuya' includes the Chinese character for 'valley', and this station is located at the region's lowest point. So intense is the activity here that it is as if most of those who come to Shibuya are being spewed out and sucked into the station. Among these droves of people are many high-school girls. They wear their school uniforms with socks scrunched right down, skirts hitched up as high as they will go and gaudily applied make-up. This area exists as the Mecca for these girls where previously it was populated by sedate-looking adults. In the 1980s commercial buildings began to appear, and it became a kids' town. At present, Shibuya is *the* place for observing the particular consumption habits of teenage girls and women in their 20s. Once they consider something to be '*kawaii*', roughly translated as 'cute', it often draws media attention. Directly in front of the station rise the arches for Center-gai (Centre street/area) with its narrow street the epitome of Shibuya-ness, brimming with teenagers.

Renma occupies the third and fourth floors of a building near the entrance of Center-gai. The interior is chic, its atmosphere so relaxed that the commotion outside seems unreal. Wood and bamboo are used to evoke both simplicity and elegance. Its scale seems small, but this creation represents the mainstream of the current Japanese aesthetic. Perhaps the establishment might fit in better in a more adult area than Shibuya – the age of the patrons is actually somewhat higher than in surrounding places, with many people over 40. The designer, Muramatsu, has a forte for creating spaces out of natural materials that ease and relax, with many elements that would not appear out of place in a dwelling. Partitioned rooms and booths have been in vogue in Tokyo's bars and restaurants, and the manager of this restaurant has advertised this feature using the catchphrase 'furtive dining' to appeal to clients who – for whatever reason – would rather visit incognito. The window side facing the station is aimed at couples and has become the restaurant's main attraction, but the place maintains a pleasant atmosphere. The client requested that partitions be placed around the restaurant, but the designer felt this would make the space feel claustrophobic so a compromise was reached whereby curtained partitions were created to give a sense of expansiveness. Since wood and bamboo are live materials, they shrink after construction. Pieces that originally fitted seamlessly together begin to get out of alignment, hence the staff must pay particular attention to maintaining the bamboo pipes; meanwhile the management has apparently come to appreciate the natural-looking interior. The restaurant serves food that is a fusion of Japanese, Chinese, Vietnamese, Italian and others. It also stocks a large selection of provincial sake and distilled spirits.

Above: **Renma Shibuya**. The designer's preferences include assembling uniformly sized waste-wood chips

Right: **Renma Shibuya**. Bamboo has been assembled to weave together a variety of patterns

Above: Renma Shibuya. From the seats facing Shibuya's 'Center-gai' area one can gaze down and observe the streets below

Right: Renma Shibuya. Slices of rock are uniformly lined up to create a wall

Above: **Renma Shibuya**. The management wanted multipurpose
partitions, but the designer selected transparent materials

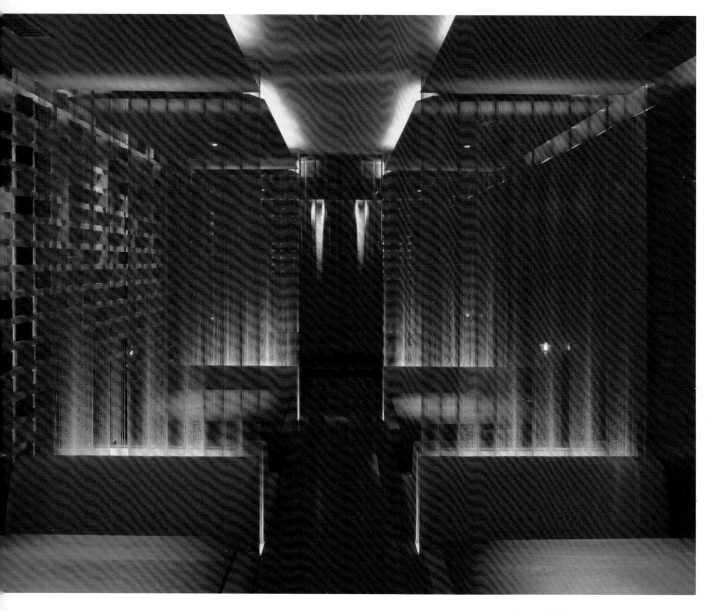

Above: **Renma Shibuya**. It is difficult to envisage such a relaxed atmosphere so close to the bustling train station

Above: **Renma Shibuya**. Utilising recycled natural
materials cuts costs

Oto Oto

Location: Glass Square, Ebisu Garden Place, Ebisu 4–20–4, Shibuya-ku
Completion date: 2003

Ryu Kosaka (Nomurakogeisha)

As you go through the entrance and gaze out across the whole restaurant, the interior seems almost like a beautiful town with rain pouring silently down. The spacious 850-square-metre premises once housed a beer-brewing facility. The actual rain that falls from the ceiling 9 metres above comes from 6,000 steel wires set at intervals approximately 6 centimetres apart. The premises include a 300-square-metre quadrilateral-shaped basement, where the entrance is situated, and if one continues on through to the side of the kitchen one goes down a level. Fanning out from here, the rectangular space measures 495 square metres vertically and forms the second level of the basement. The vertical space from the basement floor up to the ceiling in this room reaches 9 metres. Absolutely no light penetrates from outside. When Kosaka, the designer, came to look down on the space for the first time he was overwhelmed by its volume and atmosphere. He first thought to partition the space – partitioning usually goes hand in hand with Japanese interior design. Japanese partitioning differs from its Western counterpart since the Japanese utilise flexible or mobile dividers rather than solidly built ones. Even the use of a variety of screens constitutes partitioning. The idea that 'rain' might create a partition fired Kosaka's imagination, for rain holds a vital place within Japanese culture. Those familiar with Japanese prints termed *ukiyo-e* know that the artists possessed a gift for depicting rain. In particular, Kosaka drew inspiration from the prints of *ukiyo-e* artist Hiroshige Ando (1797–1858) who drew thin vertical lines to represent rain. Kosaka directly incorporated this into his design. Just as certain cultures have many terms to express familiar things – for instance, cultures in the far reaches of Alaska or Canada use some 20 different words to describe snow – so the Japanese lexicon contains many rain-related expressions, including a phrase describing rain as thread. The second level of the basement contains 6-metre-long wooden tables. Above the tables lamps with thin, bowl-shaped ceramic shades, fired in the Chinese manner, hang right down from the ceiling. An

Left: Oto Oto. The first floor entrance feels like a traditional-stye, fancy Japanese restaurant

Right: **Oto Oto**. The seats sweep across the
first level of the basement. With all the stairs
it feels like a theatre

interior that has succeeded in expressing rain to this extent stands as a rarity, for
it is an undertaking more difficult to execute than one might expect.

The second Oto Oto, it rests in the commercial compound Ebisu Garden
Place. Ebisu is an area located between the fashion districts of Shibuya and
Daikanyama, but before the Garden Place was built people only knew Ebisu as a
drab area with a beer brewery. A beer portraying Ebisu, one of the seven gods of
good fortune, on the label began to be brewed here in 1890. The brewing facilities
were brought from Germany and a station was constructed to carry the freight,
hence the location's name. Unfortunately, the gods of good fortune frowned upon
the factory, which shut its doors in 1985. Garden Place was erected on the vacant
lot of the former factory, and Sapporo Breweries Ltd, which resurrected Ebisu
Beer, runs the business. The area boasts a hotel, shops and a cinema. Oto Oto
has taken over the basement of the newest district, Glass Square, which opened
in 2002. The first Oto Oto runs out of Western Shinjuku's Centre Building and displays
an interior resembling traditional Japanese bamboo umbrellas opening. The designer
Yukio Hashimoto was the guiding light behind its design. Since the second Oto
Oto incorporates the theme of rain it makes for an interesting contrast.

Above: Oto Oto. Gauzy curtains partition the small party rooms

Left: Oto Oto. With a backdrop of falling rain one can thoroughly enjoy the Japanese exoticism

Right: Oto Oto. Table seating on stepped floors. To the right there is a display in the style of a garden, with flower bowls

Above: **Oto Oto**. A rain of vinyl-coated steel wires
pours down

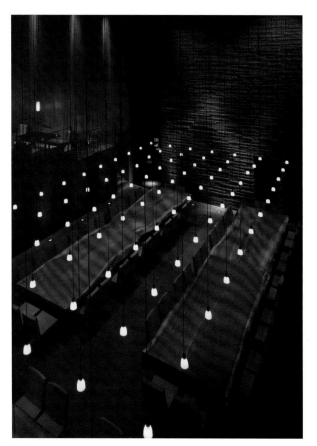

Above: **Oto Oto**. The tables in the second level of
the basement are 6 metres long. The lighting
emphasises the rain theme

Left: **Oto Oto**. From the seats in the second
level of this basement the wire rain looks like
stop-motion water droplets

Above: Oto Oto. The centre of the second level of the basement houses a display based on the image of a Japanese garden

Below: Oto Oto. Flower bowls are displayed in the garden-like space in the first level of the basement. The area below houses the kitchen of the second-level of the basement

Shinobutei Izumi

Location: Jinnan 1–19–14, Shibuya-ku
Completion date: 2002

Noritsugu Sasamori

Could one describe the style of this wonderful interior as a collage of Surrealism? It is spanned by a glass bridge that appears to float in mid-air and, below, water flows in a shallow tank. The restaurant's name, Izumi, means 'water spring' in Japanese (incidentally, Shinobutei refers to a garden where lovers rendezvous in secret). In front of the waterway lies a flat 'island' which the designer, Sasamori, calls an iceberg. In the water around this stand white birch trees. Here float several metallic boats and on these rest tables where people can be seated. It almost seems like an avant-garde rendition of *ikebana*, the traditional Japanese art of flower arrangement. The materials, elements and chromatics all contribute to a visual cacophony. Sasamori deliberately aimed for this effect while trying to evoke images of a lake in Hokkaido, the major island in the north with scenery resembling Europe rather than the stereotypical image of Japan. He believes that dining should not just be about getting nourishment, but should involve consuming fantasy. For this reason, this setting holds many clever surprises. No further explanation is necessary as this work of art speaks for itself. In 1982 Sasamori graduated from Tokai University's Architecture Department and, after working a while for Edward Suzuki, set up Atelier Toto. He not only takes on commissions for interiors but also architectural design projects. Sasamori first gained acclaim for his much talked of earlier work which includes his design of Tatou Tokyo, the sister to the celebrity hang-out Tatou New York, which opened in 1995. The floor space extends for 1,320 square metres and is fashioned after the 'guest house' design concept. Many people rent the whole place to hold parties just the way they want them. On the first floor is the main dining room, which can seat a maximum of 160 guests. Up above are balcony seats rather like the upper tiers in an opera house. One can hear the tunes of the American musicians playing on the stage. Young Japanese couples who want a little flair enjoy having 'theatre style' wedding ceremonies here.

The exterior of the Sasamori-designed Grill De Gabacho (surface area 1,779.28 square metres) looks like a rocket ship or a giant cigar-shaped UFO. Standing out in Tamagawa on the outskirts of western Tokyo the restaurant unfortunately closed, but its Western-style, all-you-can-eat buffet became popular with families who came in a spirit of playful anticipation as if they were going to Tokyo Disneyland. Med Group manages Shinobutei Izumi. Starting with a Japanese restaurant that opened in Beverly Hills, California, in 2000, this company plans, runs and produces designer restaurants. It has opened and now operates more than two dozen restaurants. Shinobutei projects the overlying concept – a space for adults to rendezvous. Each of these restaurants features a different theme. Joining the boom in restaurants with individual rooms, Sasamori also designed the Shinobutei Hotaru in Ebisu, a restaurant that showcases spherical rooms for small parties.

Above: Shinobutei Izumi. The interior as seen from the entrance. The water flows through a 15-metre waterway

Above: Shinobutei Izumi. The small space easily lends itself to an intimate atmosphere

Above: **Shinobutei Izumi**. Water, white birch trees and a metallic boat seat

Below: **Shinobutei Izumi**. The boat seats are at the top of these stairs. On the right there is a platform that portrays an iceberg

Above: **Shinobutei Izumi**. A small party room, shaped like a steel boat, with red floor-seating. The space seats groups of young revellers

Above: **Shinobutei Izumi**. The mezzanine seating far inside the restaurant

Above: **Shinobutei Izumi**. Floor-seating as seen from the boat seats

Right: **Shinobutei Izumi**. It is not only couples who sit in the small party rooms. Businessmen use them for negotiations.

Above: Shinobutei Izumi. Watch out for your head – the ceiling in the mezzanine is low. This is a common feature in Tokyo restaurants with small party rooms

Below: Shinobutei Izumi. A small party room in an S-shape stands to the rear of the premises

Seiryumon Ueno

Address: Ueno 4–4–5, Taito-ku
Completion date: 2002

En-ma

This Chinese restaurant is located in Ueno, which has a large train terminal. The area's buildings are densely crammed together and Ueno still evokes the atmosphere of Japan immediately after the Second World War. An assortment of large and small stores is squeezed together beneath the elevated railway tracks. Clothes and foodstuffs are for sale cut price, a reminder that Ueno was once a squalid place of black-market operators and dubious enterprises. Today the streets still brim with shoppers. In particular, the shopping area known as Ameyoko resembles Hong Kong in that once you get on to the walkways you are guided back to a labyrinth of small stores without so much as the floorspace of an automobile. It stirs up images of the Kowloon Walled City that was a feature of Hong Kong before it reverted to the People's Republic of China. Aluminium Chinese characters are affixed to the otherwise simple exterior of Seiryumon's narrow building which is clad in aluminium chequered plate. Coming in by way of the entrance facing the main street, you can see a faint light emanating from the recesses of the subtle darkness. It's dim on the first floor where a blue light seeps out from under the flooring. Round tables flaunt designs that make one think of tattoos or old-fashioned kimonos (of the kind that became the pattern for aloha shirts). It's almost as if it were a modern-day opium den. There are also four tables on the mezzanine where many steel cables encircle the space, and it looks as though giant lotus leaves are floating in the air. The patrons who occupy the store's lotus seats appear to become lotus eaters. The ambience of the third floor is slightly different to that of those mysterious spaces. Its green walls and box seats lend it a tranquil air.

The restaurant's design was handled by En-ma design office, a firm whose forte is the production of temporary spaces mostly for car and computer exhibition stands. They have gained a reputation for dynamic and glitzy creations. The company's art director, Yasuaki Kanau, designed this project, basing it on ideas derived from a type of *feng shui* aesthetic. He comments on the space saying: 'This is a monolith within this bustling area, a lair for the dragon that appears in Chinese mythology. Several rooms unfold within, there is an enticing garden, and mysterious butterflies gather. The people seduced by the lair become butterflies as well. Here and there lotus leaves open, people unwind, and for a fleeting moment forget the harsh realities of the real world while they enjoy home-style cuisine from Taiwan.' Soho's Hospitality Group manages the restaurant. They run not only such high-profile venues as Nobu's Tokyo restaurant, but also a variety of both large and small establishments, each with a different designer, their innovative decor leaving the restaurant-goer amazed. Seiryumon also has eight other stores in the vicinity of Tokyo, with the Seiryumon in Setagaya especially worth checking out.

Below: **Seiryumon Ueno**. Asian-style motifs sprawl across the tables and bring to mind Japanese tattoos

Above: Seiryumon Ueno. The entire restaurant boasts the theme of a 'dragon's lair', following *feng shui* ideals

Above left: Seiryumon Ueno. The interior has a floating feeling

Above right: Seiryumon Ueno. The third floor with plant-like motifs

Right: Seiryumon Ueno. The third floor box seats have a relaxed, Art Deco-style ambience

Above left: Seiryumon Ueno. The simple exterior. Originally, there were plans to plate it with shiny silver metal

Above right: Seiryumon Ueno. The exotic, Chinese-style entrance. Flower motifs appear throughout much of the interior

Left: Seiryumon Ueno. Patterns of fantasy-world butterflies are projected on to the walls

Right: Seiryumon Ueno. Dining on the first floor or mezzanine feels like riding on cloud-borne lotus leaves

J-Pop Cafe Odaiba

Location: Odaiba 1–6–1, Minato-ku
Completion date: 2002

Katsunori Suzuki

With beautiful lines running throughout the interior, this store is nostalgically futuristic, recalling a spaceship out of an old science-fiction book. Katsunori Suzuki designed the space by reappraising Art Nouveau's plant-like motifs while paying optimistic homage to a new form. This is evident in his use of biotechnology to create a futuristic image. He feels a repugnance for typical Modernism and Minimalism, aiming instead for a colourful and fun, toy-like, jellybean style. Katsunori draws his inspiration from the cartoons that many of his generation saw as youngsters and pays homage to such designers as Verner Panton and Luigi Colani. The facade is independent with a luminescent wall in which are set green spheres that light up to represent eggs, expressing the tiniest units of life. This green is made from neon and stays the same colour. There are approximately 1,700 spheres, and to reduce the cost the spheres were custom-manufactured in China. The space is mostly made from gypsum and hemp fibres, its components factory-made and assembled on site. The light materials that make up the skeleton for the space are relatively sturdy and have a coating to enhance flexibility. Inside there is almost no colour – only a computer-controlled LED lighting system in place to change the interior's hue. Every seat is equipped with a customised system allowing patrons to enjoy music videos selected at will. They can also hold small concerts from a stage with a large monitor.

The J-Pop Cafe is situated in the Tokyo Joypolis video arcade in the commercial district of Odaiba. Odaiba is on the Tokyo waterfront and during the Bubble Economy it acted as a magnet for many large companies which planned to redevelop it as a subcentre of the city. The café's opening was scheduled to coincide with the 1996 World City Expo Tokyo, but as the Bubble Economy burst, the city abandoned many of the plans. However, it is still a media centre with a number of office buildings and a TV station. It draws a large number of visitors from Tokyo as well, with its large shopping malls, entertainment districts, hot spring baths and a waterfront park where windsurfing is on offer. Despite the Post-Modern frills of Odaiba's architecture the area is also of historical significance. The name 'Odaiba' means 'the place for cannon bulwarks' and derives from the fact that it is here that the Edo shogunate rushed to construct armed defences on the bay when Commodore Matthew Perry came with his 'black ships' in 1853. He carried papers proposing a commercial and friendship treaty with the Japanese emperor, bringing to an end Japan's isolationist stance. That era seems a far cry from today's Odaiba where establishments such as the J-Pop Cafe push the envelope with daring new designs and technology.

Above: J-Pop Cafe Odaiba. The exterior, with its rubber balls, brings to mind the inner systems of an organism

Right: J-Pop Cafe Odaiba. A shop by the entrance near the Joypolis video arcade

Above: **J-Pop Cafe Odaiba**. The seats are the interior designer's beloved Panton chairs

Above: **J-Pop Cafe Odaiba**. The restaurant area commands a superb view of Tokyo Bay's waterfront

Above: **J-Pop Cafe Odaiba**. Looking out from the stage in the direction of fast-food counters

Left: **J-Pop Cafe Odaiba**. A big screen plays music videos of Japanese pop music, so-called J-Pop

Right: **J-Pop Cafe Odaiba**. The design looks part-robot, part-mollusc. Using a single tone for the floor, walls and ceiling makes the interior feel colourless

Left: **J-Pop Cafe Odaiba**. The facade lies at the end of a long passageway

Below: **J-Pop Cafe Odaiba**. A service counter in the fast-food area

Right: **J-Pop Cafe Odaiba**. Beyond circular windows one sees the fast-food area. The wall next to the tables has built-in liquid crystal monitors

Below: **J-Pop Cafe Odaiba**. The box seats of the restaurant area are raised a step up from the floor

SHOP

Fashion truly came into its own in the mid-1980s with the second generation of postwar designers who had emerged in the 1970s. Issey Miyake, Kenzo Takada, Kansai Yamamoto, Rei Kawakubo and Yohji Yamamoto, all of whom had worked on the international scene, now began to make headway in the domestic market. The designers and brands that emerged at this time are too numerous to mention but the interior design of their shops became more individualised. Young people's fervour for fashion peaked just before 1990, after which it began to decline. Fashion became more casual and streetwear more prominent as design moved towards homogenisation. At one extreme, many brands fell by the wayside while luxury brands became concentrated in the famous foreign fashion houses. Low-price brands began to expand, and among them UNIQLO grew to the point of being dubbed 'the national outfit'. It seems fashion has polarised between these two extremes.

In the Japanese commercial world called 'the backstreets of Harajuku', the area known for its multitude of fashion-related outlets, designers build brands aimed at the young consumer. In this particular market, merchandise pours out, fiercely competing to attract fashion-savvy young domestic

customers. You can see from the example of illustrated cotton print T-shirts that can fetch as much as several hundred dollars a piece that product information has become the value of the products. This is a system in which shop designs have their own world, and many shop owners create their own interiors as well. The international brands with business operations in Tokyo such as Hermès, Prada, Dior and Vuitton, build large-scale stores under the direction of eminent designers and continue to garner high earnings despite the present economic downturn. The Japanese show an enormous enthusiasm for, and devotion to, brand-name products in more than simply fashion. The Japanese market is peculiar in that a wide range of people purchase big-name brands, so this form of shopping doesn't necessarily reflect their income level, something for which Tokyo offers infinite examples. There is in Tokyo a group of brand-name acolytes who drive Mercedes-Benzes yet live in shabby apartments, or who get by on low incomes but take on extra work in the form of hard physical labour in order to buy their much desired Hermès Birkin handbags.

This passion for brand-name goods also relates to the diversity of the consumers described in David Brooks' book, *Bobos in Paradise* (2000). One could call it the cutting edge of capitalist consumer style and a phenomenon that should be taken as a new trend. It is not something to be dismissed as only showing the lack of principles among consumers. Present-day brands will no longer target a limited social class. This devotion to brands and Japanese consumer trends make strategies for brand development that are successful in provincial European cities apply equally to Japan.

Below: **Q ❤ Flagship Ebisu-nishi**. With the theme of 'Casa', the shop was made to look like different areas in a domestic house. This section alludes to a terrace

APC Underground

Location: Jingumae 4–27–6, Shibuya-ku
Completion date: 2002

Laurent Deroo

After studying history and linguistics at the Sorbonne in Paris, Jean Touitou wandered around South America for a year before setting up APC, which stands for Atelier de Production et de Creation. At first the brand name gave no indication that Touitou appreciates fashion's semiotic *raison d'être*. From its inception the business channelled its energies into the mail-order side of the operation, which shows their grasp of Jean Baudrillard's concept of fashion as symbol: *'simulacre'* – people fall in love with images rather than with the real thing.

To reach the store you leave Harajuku station and go through the bustling bazaar-like Takeshita Street. Arriving at the avenue Meijidori, you cross the street and go down a short way to find APC located in a basement. Fashion aficionados frequent these backstreets of Harajuku and in a press release Touitou comments on the area saying, 'Young people gather in Harajuku, and while everyone comes here once they hit a certain age, once they pass a certain age they migrate elsewhere. However, it's a place that everyone has been to at least once. At my age people start to lose interest in young people so it's always important to be near young people. In this sense having a shop here has significance.' Gravel is laid out at the foot of the stairs and the entrance sits atop a wooden deck. With an elevation entirely encased in glass, part of the interior sticks through as if flying out of the glass wall. The space is divided with the shop on the right and a wooden stage-like space occupying the left.

In the centre of the store is a rail affixed to the ceiling to which support panels are attached. Depending on how they are assembled, the panels can become display shelves or fitting rooms. The interior brings to mind a gallery rather than just a shop, and director Sofia Coppola used the space to film the Tokyo party scene for her film *Lost in Translation* (2003). The space would also look perfectly natural as a bar.

Laurent Deroo, the architect who led this project, has previously designed film sets. Here his design drew inspiration from Second World War era bunkers found on the shores of Normandy as well as borrowing from images of war and student activism. At the same time, his designs also incorporate the concept of 'the stage'. Just as backstage in a theatre, the staff place clothing behind curving wooden walls so that one can see the clothes from outside through the glass.

Above: **APC Underground**. A restaurant formerly occupied the space. Ripping off the previous wall coverings left an interesting texture so the designer tried his best to leave it exposed

Above: **APC Underground**. The panelling
doubles as a partition

Above: **APC Underground**. The shop and stage
have been divided into two distinct areas

Left: **APC Underground**. Absolutely no
merchandise has been put on the wooden stage

Above: APC Underground. The panelling can be used to form a shelving unit, and can also create a fitting room

Above: APC Underground. View of the panels when they are shut

Above: APC Underground. The area around the
sales desk

Left: APC Underground. The wall as viewed
from the sales area. Lighting has been affixed
to the slit above

Above: APC Underground. Peeping into the shop's interior from the wooden wall outside

Right: APC Underground. When looked at from outside, a portion of the wooden wall appears to fly out from the premises

Y's Roppongi Hills

Location: Roppongi 6–12–4, Minato-ku
Completion date: 2003

Ron Arad

In the early 1970s, Yohji Yamamoto and Rei Kawakubo won acclaim for their iconoclastic breaking down of pre-existing notions of clothing. Flying in the face of the ideal Westerners had constructed of appropriate attire and the way clothing should look, they took their inspiration from the vagabond and the drifter, incorporating into their work the chaotic and the alternative in terms of fabric, line and colour, assimilating into their vision Japanese philosophy in the form of materials and shapes. It might be called an Asian countermovement to the Western fashion establishment. Even today Yamamoto has international standing as a fashion designer. This Roppongi outlet serves as the special store for Y's, the brand he established in 1972. In order to select his designer Yamamoto searched the world of architects and designers and eventually chose Rod Arad in order to break with what had hitherto been the image of shop design.

The shop premises extend 530 square metres and feature three large structural columns. Arad had originally intended to conceal these columns, but he discovered something more appropriate in the form of parking-lot turntables. Due to chronic lack of space, Tokyo requires three-dimensional parking lots. These parking lots make use of turntables that rotate the direction of the automobile. Arad added one fake column as well and installed turntables in the lower portion of the four columns. The speed of rotation of each column can be increased or decreased. Thirty-four Italian-made aluminium loops coil around the sides of each pillar up to the ceiling and have a device which allows them to rotate 360 degrees, turning them into 'sculptures' which revolve. If shelving boards are attached to a loop, it can also display merchandise. He also designed the register counter to look like a pillar to create an illusion of lightness and movement in the space.

Although at first glance it seems simple, Shiro Nakata took on this deceptively complex construction and worked as the project's on-site architect. Arad and Nakata exchanged ideas via e-mail and evolved their construction plan together.

Prior to acquiring these premises, Yohji Yamamoto had often employed static, simple and Minimal styles in his shops' interiors; this store stands in complete contrast. As this shop is special, so it becomes the place of transmission for the cultural image of the brand. In 2002, he began various new ventures such as his prêt-à-porter collection Y's Paris. This interior embodies the entwining of the brand's art and philosophy with Yamamoto's challenging spirit. Unusually for such top-end stores in Japan, Y's Roppongi Hills also carries exclusive merchandise such as one-of-a-kind handmade knitwear.

Above: **Y's Roppongi Hills.** The new store concept encapsulates Yohji Yamamoto's orientation towards art

Right: **Y's Roppongi Hills.** The speed at which the pillars rotate can be controlled, and they can be made to revolve at quite a velocity

Above: **Y's Roppongi Hills.** Y's colourful logo on the exterior looks hand-drawn. Even at this point one can see that this outlet differs from the concept of previous Y's stores, making it a unique venture

Above: **Y's Roppongi Hills**. Merchandise can be hung from the loops while boards can be sandwiched between the loops to create shelves

Above: **Y's Roppongi Hills**. The looped columns can express a variety of shapes

Right: **Y's Roppongi Hills**. The use of red for the counter is striking amongst the white walls and grey pillars. The designer aimed to create an ambient light within the store

Above: **Y's Roppongi Hills**. The counter also
emphasises horizontal lines to match the
column 'sculpture'

Left: **Y's Roppongi Hills**. Each loop is assembled from two parts. The extended loops are attached to a column made up of 34 circular loops

Above: **Y's Roppongi Hills**. The glass wall on the street, Keyaki Dori, has a rounded, half-cylinder surface

Louis Vuitton Roppongi Hills

Location: Roppongi 6–12–3, Minato-ku
Completion date: 2003

Jun Aoki, Aurelio Clementi and Eric Carlson

Jun Aoki took on the exterior design of the world's largest Louis Vuitton store, which opened in New York City in February 2004. Before this he had designed both the interior and exterior of the Roppongi Hills store. Roppongi Hills stands alongside Ginza and Omotesando as the area with the highest concentration of upscale-brand stores. Aoki might be called the man responsible for the face of Vuitton. Before he took charge of the facade design of the Manhattan store, he had also designed the exterior of the Omotesando Vuitton (which used to boast the world's largest sales floorspace) as well as the Vuitton franchise exterior of Ginza's Matsuya department store. For the Roppongi Hills project Aoki worked closely with two other designers, and after half a year of discussion they worked out the store's design and concept including the position of the sales floor and the way the merchandise would be displayed.

Situated near the centre of Keyakizaka Street, an avenue lined with internationally famous brands, along with its neighbours this store has a special cachet as a shop that can only be found here. Differing from the Omotesando store, with its characteristic stacked-up trunks motif symbolic of Vuitton, the Roppongi store instead has a restrained translucence achieved with thousands of glass pipes that measure 10 centimetres in diameter and 30 centimetres in length. The effect is to make the exterior literally shine out on the surroundings while reflecting the variety of the city's lights. Also, there is a mechanism to display the brand logo (best viewed from across the street at night). Appropriately for Tokyo consumers' cutting-edge nightlife district, the store is open until 9 pm on most days, but until 11 pm on Thursday, Friday and Saturday. Many people continue to shop right up to closing time.

Aoki draws on Roland Barthes' theory of Japan expressed in *L'Empire des signes (Empire of Signs)*, a work that discusses at length the Japanese culture of wrapping. In conversation with the author, Aoki commented: 'Barthes argues that the centre of Tokyo, the Imperial Palace, becomes a vacuum region that traffic avoids. So to speak, the place is a zero. Barthes points out that this is something seen in many things thought of as Japan-like, but fashion in itself is superficial in a sense, and wraps around many people, and the core of this is zero as well. However, people must be clad in something from fashion in their everyday life.' One can read the shop in this way: this building is a wrapped-up gift, the brand prepared for its customers. In the interior are collected metallic circular rings that have the same 10-centimetre diameter as the glass tubes and these rings emit a sense of lightness. They highlight the decor over the space. Through translucency, solidity and reflectivity they have produced a sense of infinite scale and succeed in drawing out the brand's new image.

Above: Louis Vuitton Roppongi Hills. 30,000 glass tubes help make up the exterior, through which the letters of the store name can be seen. This is especially attractive at night

Right: Louis Vuitton Roppongi Hills. The first floor as seen from the middle of the staircase

Below: Louis Vuitton Roppongi Hills. Movable display cases along the back counter on the first floor

Above: **Louis Vuitton Roppongi Hills**. In Japan, Vuitton has become a brand of the utmost popularity and visibility. When the store held its grand opening many people queued up outside throughout the night

Below: **Louis Vuitton Roppongi Hills**. The sales area for leather bags on the second floor

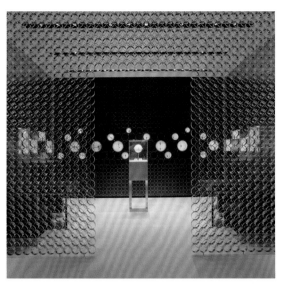

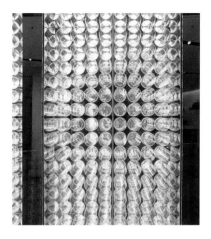

Left: Louis Vuitton Roppongi Hills. The watch and jewellery sales area features mounted stainless-steel rings on a leather-covered wall

Above and below: Louis Vuitton Roppongi Hills. Detail of the glass tubes. They aid the partitioning of the store, into areas such as this one for ladies' shoes

Below: **Louis Vuitton Roppongi Hills**. A fibre-optic video projection system is fixed on the risers of the stairway

Below: **Louis Vuitton Roppongi Hills**. The
interior has a complex intersection of
stairways and dead ends

Miss Sixty Meijidori

Location: Jingumae 6–25–14, Shibuya-ku
Completion date: 2003

Studio 63

This Italian brand mainly features the type of denim casual wear that is particularly popular in Europe and the United States. With its base in Chieti, Italy, this brand makes prominent use of SPA (Specialty Store Retailer of Private Label Apparel), and designs clothes mostly for people in their 20s and with a retro nod to the styles seen in American films from the 1950s to the 1980s. This store stands as the brand's Japanese flagship, becoming its third and largest Asian outpost following the opening of two shops in Hong Kong. The design of this store comes from the Florentine designers in Studio 63 who are responsible for the brand's brilliant shops around the world. For this project they joined forces with Japanese designers among whom was Kouji Sakai. He has experience in store design for Italian brands, and has been involved in Miss Sixty's projects since they set up their Hong Kong showroom. For this shop they faithfully reproduced Studio 63's style.

Normally, in order to establish branding, visual consistency is necessary but some brands have realised that consumers have tired of this approach. Rather than lay out all their stores to the same format Miss Sixty dropped much of the standardised appearance, opting instead to emphasise the creation of a design that fits the city's image. With no set pattern for this brand's stores, it becomes a fitting showcase for the respective cultures of the world's cities. Among the stores, the Tokyo one especially brims with energy.

Located along the avenue Meijidori almost midway between Harajuku and Shibuya, the design concept is a 'theatre'. Inspiration came from 1960s and 1970s fashion and includes some experimental elements as well. The merging of the boutique with a café becomes the distinctive feature of this store. Even after the store closes the café stays open and has spaces that can be used as a theatre and a gallery. Yoshiyuki Morii, who has made a name in this niche market, took on the design of the café.

One often sees cafés adjoining boutiques. In Tokyo it has become fashionable to make shops that fuse two types of business, such as restaurants with nail salons. Stores that hold musical or cinema events have increased too. Boutiques have moved from an era in which they simply sold clothes to promoting and selling things from the whole cultural gamut. Rather than buying a CD at a megastore chain, the customer gains a sense of added value when purchasing something in a space he or she actively enjoys. Broadly speaking, all the merchandise could be included under the umbrella of fashion.

Above: **Miss Sixty Meijidori**. Enormous projection screens help to transform the store into a stage

Right: **Miss Sixty Meijidori**. Each area has its own expressive qualities

Below: **Miss Sixty Meijidori**. The café is open from 8 am until 11 pm

Above: **Miss Sixty Meijidori**. The display area just
inside the entrance on the left

Above: **Miss Sixty Meijidori**. Curtained fitting rooms are situated behind four metallic rooms

Right: **Miss Sixty Meijidori**. The shop design of Miss Sixty outlets fits the culture of the relevant cities. This store was positioned between the two hubs of youth culture: Harajuku and Shibuya

Top left: **Miss Sixty Meijidori**. The interior overflows with a youthful vivaciousness that suits the brand

Bottom left: **Miss Sixty Meijidori**. The cashiers work at the green counter in the centre

Above: **Miss Sixty Meijidori**. View of the inside
of the fitting rooms

Above: **Miss Sixty Meijidori**. The wall decorations
have a disco-kitsch appeal

Left: **Miss Sixty Meijidori**.
The brand christened the first
Japanese store, its largest in Asia,
as the flagship

Above: **Miss Sixty Meijidori**. Even after closing time the interior has a café-like atmosphere

Right: **Miss Sixty Meijidori**. The shop merges with the café which sports 1960s- and 1970s-style design

Q ♥ Flagship Ebisu-nishi

Location: Ebisu-nishi 1-30-10, Shibuya-ku
Completion date: 2003

Masamichi Katayama

As the subsidiary of the famous and longstanding Ginza tailor Yamagataya, Q is managed and developed by Sympathy. The shop name Q stands for 'Queen' and the business promotes itself as a girly and casual speciality boutique aimed at women from their late 20s up. The shop featured here is situated in west Ebisu in the fashion hub known as Daikanyama.

Masamichi Katayama of Wonderwall fashioned the shop's interior. Katayama works his shop design wizardry here with such items as sneakers and T-shirts, adorning his showcases and displays so as to render the merchandise intensely alluring, transcending their existence as mere sneakers and T-shirts the moment they are illuminated. The space is filled with a mysterious light creating an aura reminiscent of science fiction. The shops he creates seem like modern-age phantasmagoria. Katayama stands as one of the foremost designers to decisively and faithfully represent what Tokyo style is all about.

In 1992, Katayama set up H Design Associates with Tsutomu Kurokawa. They turned out interior and furniture design that drew much acclaim from fashion designers and editors. After H Design dissolved Katayama set up the design company Wonderwall as well as the merchandise development company Anotherwall. His design work extends beyond shop design to encompass lighting, furniture and the Le Corbusier-inspired Cigarro 2000 personal computer. Katayama says that his future dream is to design a hotel.

Katayama himself has an inordinate love of shopping and his office displays, in garage sale fashion, a cavalcade of figures, instruments, books and a miscellany of other items that fanatics would surely covet. It seems as if he holds the key to deftly grasping the shopper's psyche. He embodies this age and can construct the environment to showcase things people instinctively want. This capacity hits home with today's consumers and has the power to lure them in.

The shop incorporates the theme 'Casa' with an interior envisioned as a stylish manor. The store divides into a grassy entrance, a dining room with a sizeable table, and a living room with a sofa. The design concept aims to get people to shop while they look around the house. The greater portion of the store focuses on pieces from the brands of new designers making their first showing in Japan, while the first level of the basement showcases specialist items that buyers have purchased around the world.

Above: **Q**. The night view of the facade

Right: **Q**. A paper screen made out of a pattern using the letter Q

Above: **Q**. Designers often utilise innovative hanging
displays

Above left: **Q**. The design effectively mixes the casual
with the sumptuous

Above right: **Q**. The entrance is beyond the stairway

Right: **Q**. The walls around the
stairway have a feeling of warmth

Left: **Q**. Where people would dine in the 'Casa'

Top right: **Q**. It is tempting to put one's feet up and relax in this area resembling a living room

Bottom right: **Q**. This store is Q's flagship, but it has a franchise in the Shibuya department store, Parco, also designed by Katayama

United Bamboo

Location: Sarugaku-cho 20-14, Shibuya-ku
Completion date: 2003

Vito Acconci

A man known for poetry, performing and instrumentation in the 1960s, Vito Acconci, who has recently garnered acclaim for the novel architecture of the glass-encased walkway in the Project for Mur River in Graz, Austria, designed his first shop in Tokyo for the New York brand United Bamboo. His previous creations include the louvred walkway in Shibuya's commercial complex, Mark City, which won him fans in Japan. In 1998, Japanese-born Miho Aoki, who studied fashion at New York's FIT, joined forces with Vietnamese-born Thuy O Pham, who studied architecture at Cooper Union, to create United Bamboo. Since they haven't set up a shop in the US yet, this is the world's first United Bamboo store. What was previously a company's dormitory, a building of lightweight concrete and steel beams, was refurbished. The ground level makes up the shop, and the upper floor is the office. On the first floor the glass facade bulges into the store while on the second floor it bulges out. A computer-linked monitor showcases images of the brand's promotional video. The interior uses elastic PVC (polyvinyl chloride) sheets, a material also used in video projection screens, as a skin to cover the walls, ceiling and shelves. Inside fluorescent lamps are evenly placed on the existing walls. The light diffuses and is cast on the surfaces and clothing. The interior looks like a cavern or valley emitting white light, and it also looks like a forest of oversized bamboo. Wall surfaces and ceiling panels are partitioned, making it easier to maintain the interior than might appear. Hanging rods curve down and are pressed and flattened into vertical stands that bend perdendicularly, each with an iPod holding headphones. United Bamboo also vends CDs since it sells a lifestyle concept that goes hand in hand with the clothes. This shop is in Daikanyama, the most style-conscious area of Tokyo and the place of origin for many Tokyo fashions. Even though the foreign media mostly focus on Harajuku, in actuality the Japanese consider Daikanyama to be much more sophisticated. In this neighbourhood a striking sense of contrast to this avant-garde boutique comes from a sneaker shop and a restaurant remodelled from an old wooden dwelling. Since the store is positioned near a residential district it has quite a presence at night. If you look at the glowing light it casts off in these environs, it is apparent that Acconci's creation is not only a commercial venture but also a work of art.

Above: **United Bamboo**. The light diffuses on to surfaces and shows off merchandise

Below: **United Bamboo** A slanted hanging rod

Right: **United Bamboo** A niche-like space

Below: **United Bamboo** The interior uses elastic polyvinyl chloride sheets that need `careful maintenance

Opposite: **United Bamboo** The small elegant
maze of the interior

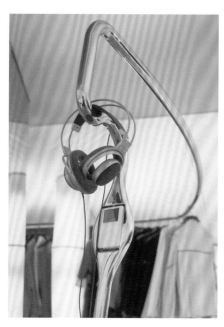

Below: **United Bamboo** The light shines
out creating a sci-fi atmosphere here

Right: **United Bamboo** A steel hanging rod
with a built-in iPod

Left: United Bamboo
The interior is reminiscent of a forest of bamboo

Right: United Bamboo
A sales counter

Below: United Bamboo
The sliding door at the entrance is an unusual curved shape

Above: **United Bamboo** The night view of the
exterior impresses shoppers and passers-by

WORK

In Japan, the company hierarchy paradigm that based promotion on seniority has weakened as more women have come to take management positions, and there is a feeling that the labour structure in companies has begun to alter. But the fact of the matter is that the majority of corporations do not change their ways overnight. Even in large companies with international profiles the internal workings often remain old-fashioned and most offices have the old, tiresome layout of desks lined up in an open-plan space. Usually there aren't even individual rooms. However, with the IT revolution of recent years offices have increasingly been forced to change, and reduce their superfluous contents. For example, the administrative staff of a restaurant management company has just one large table with chairs. Armed with only their mobile phones and laptop computers, employees move about and sit anywhere they please to do their jobs. Prior to the IT revolution, it would have been impossible to see this sight in any Japanese corporation. As change continues to affect companies' approach both to how they operate and to their public face, the number of places where the work of exceptional interior designers is sought should increase correspondingly.

In recent years, businesses have begun to realise that design reaches beyond the product and also has a profound effect in moulding a company image that appeals to consumers. Concentrated predominantly in foreign-affiliated companies or in industries such as advertising and publishing that are sensitive to the changes of the times, offices and workspaces that take

Work

design into consideration have increased, and the showrooms of such businesses have rapidly become high-end. The spaces shown in this section make up only a very small proportion of them.

Changing offices and their design allows for a re-evaluation of a company's internal working, rearranging it and making things more efficient. A backlash might occur within the company, but if this can be contained the operation becomes increasingly dynamic.

Above: **Shu Uemura Atelier**. This motif seems to have been inspired by plants. Henri Gueydan, who designed the project, claims that the experience he most benefited from as an architect was growing vegetables

Beacon Communications Office

Location: Shinagawa-ku
Completion date: 2002

Klein Dytham Architecture

In 2001 Leo Burnett merged with the Japanese branch of D'Arcy, with a 34 per cent investment by Dentsu, and Beacon Communications was born. It is affiliated to Publicis SA, the world's fourth largest advertising agency. About 300 people work in this office, which occupies the 11th to the 14th floors of an office building that straddles Japan Rail's Yamanote line.

One floor extends 60 metres by 15 metres with no internal columns and each level is designed according to a target consumer with separate floors dedicated to family, men, women and community. The materials, colours and furniture differ on each floor. For example, the family floor has a purple theme and makes use of wooden materials while the men's floor comes in hues of blue and uses stainless steel. Pink covers the women's floor with snakeskin patterns adorning several places, and the community floor is done out in green. The core area of each floor integrates meeting rooms, printing rooms, chat spaces, kitchens, merchandise-testing areas and communal spaces. A large ribbon-like surface envelops these areas. This structural 'ribbon' descends from the ceiling and slithers down to the floor. By functioning both as wall and floor it expresses a sense of movement. Hence the design has quite a playful sense to it.

The meeting rooms and conference areas are see-through, a transparency that echoes the absence of individual spaces; even the executives and president do not have private offices. People take their laptops and work at the massive tables, making for an office environment that transcends what was previously thinkable for conventional Japanese workplaces. Offices that prioritise creative jobs will probably come to resemble this.

At Beacon Communications they create brand project teams, but they can also fashion the spaces in which teams interact. The 11th floor houses a beauty salon and a lounge called the Agency Forum, while the 13th has a British-style pub. Employees can also cook in a kitchen located on the 14th floor. As in this case, corporations that produce superior brands have a genuine appreciation of the value of design when it comes to skilfully branding themselves.

This page and opposite: **Beacon Communications Office**. The reception area and corridor of the 'community' floor

Above: **Beacon Communications Office**. The
conference room on the 12th floor

Left: **Beacon Communications Office**. The
'family' floor library. The facilities include a kitchen to
test merchandise

Above and left: **Beacon Communications Office**.
The symbolic colour of the 'men's' floor is blue

Above: **Beacon Communications Office**. The
workspace on the 'community' floor

Above: Beacon Communications Office. The British pub on the 13th floor. The products of a Scotch-producing client are always on display. In recent years, many corporations have equipped their buildings with rooms like this, to entertain clients

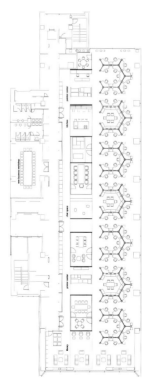

Left: Beacon Communications Office. Floor plan

Top and middle right: **Beacon Communications Office**. The 'family' space on the 14th floor

Bottom right and opposite: **Beacon Communications Office**. The 'women's' floor with its telltale colour scheme of pink with snakeskin accents. Could this somehow be a veiled reference to Eve in the Bible?

Shu Uemura Atelier

Location: Aoyama
Completion date: 2003

CRC – Henri Gueydan + Fumiko Kaneko

Executed in maisonette style, this space was designed to serve as an occasional small-scale retreat atelier for Shu Uemura. In the 1950s, Shu Uemura became the first Japanese to work as a make-up artist in Hollywood. He set up a line of cosmetics bearing his name in 1967 and eventually went on to open shops in 23 countries. In 2003 his brand became a subsidiary of France's L'Oréal, the world's largest cosmetics producer, and the brand continues to develop worldwide. The office of Japanese Fumiko Kaneko and Frenchman Henri Gueydan, Ciel Rouge Creation (CRC), took on this project which required the remodelling of an expensive, leased residence in Aoyama. The pair had previously undertaken commercial architecture work for Shu Uemura, including interior projects such as shops and showrooms, and they had also built a variety of structures including dwellings, kindergartens and factories while expanding their realm of activity to France, Korea and Taiwan.

Trees were visible from the southern window of the original Aoyama space, but since in itself the room was rather bland and lacked elegance, the designers got rid of the existing ceiling and boards, and covered what was revealed with a completely new surface into which they embedded various shapes. They brought the space together with orange, a colour seldom used in Japan, in order to absorb the light coming in from the terrace so that the interior didn't glare. The round windows express the notion that this place is a 'hole', a concept they kept in mind during the design process, creating, 'a "hole" that simply feels comfortable to be in with an organic and sensual warmth to it'. According to Kaneko, the white elements visible in the shelves, sofa, circular counter, arc-shaped lighting, circular office desk, circular stairway and make-up stand work together to give the place a sense of volume while providing accents. The colour white is the signature of Shu Uemura the artist, while the designers emphasise the interior of the room with a line – organic lines are their own signature feature.

Above: **Shu Uemura Atelier**. The atelier shows the designers' characteristically organic and futuristic sensibilities

Top right: **Shu Uemura Atelier**. All the shelves are built-in

Bottom right: **Shu Uemura Atelier**. The project refurbished a luxury condominium along a tranquil residential block in Aoyama

Top right: **Shu Uemura Atelier**. A subtle orange colour, a rare choice for decoration in Japan, adorns the walls. The designer drew inspiration from a photo of scenery that he found in a magazine

Bottom right: **Shu Uemura Atelier**. A circular mirror in the middle of the arc-shaped lighting creates an optical illusion

Above: **Shu Uemura Atelier**.
A room in the incredibly plain residence. The pre-existing walls and ceiling are now covered with panelling

Left: **Shu Uemura Atelier**.
Around the spiral staircase. There is space to take a catnap at the top of the stairs

Above: Shu Uemura Atelier. Arcs are used
throughout the design and seem to echo each other

Above: **Shu Uemura Atelier**. The atelier is used for prep meetings and unwinding

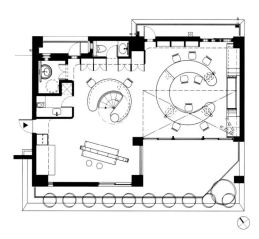

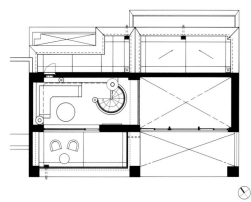

Left and above: **Shu Uemura Atelier**. Floor plans

Trans Building Office and Gallery

Location: Ebisu-minami 2–12–19, Shibuya-ku
Completion date: 2002

Yukiharu Takematsu + EPA

The juxtaposition of the beehive-shaped frame with the honeycomb glass of this office/gallery in Ebisu reminds one of Aoyama's Prada, but actually this building was erected first. At first glance there is nothing overt about the Trans Building to suggest a total experiment in construction as with the Prada store, but in fact it is a showcase for innovation. Nor is this only a feat of construction; it involves enveloping the building with a material in the manner of a shell. The shell had to be appropriate for the space and it also meant that the interior, which was designed afterwards, could not be a straightforward design. The honeycomb glass that makes up the building membrane fulfils the dual role of providing light as well as temperature control. Since it insulates the place well there is no need for heating, and since the glass reduces sunlight in the summer just a little air conditioning is sufficient. However, during the few hours that sunshine does pour in, the place is deluged with light so bright that unless the staff use blinds, they have to wear sunglasses.

The above-ground first floor and first level of the basement serve as spaces to display modern sculpture while a graphic design company operates out of the second and third floors. Yukihara Takematsu took on the construction of this building. After studying at London's Branson Coates Architecture School he set up the EPA (Environmental Protection Architecture) Institute in 1991. It was a time when few businesses incorporated environmental policies, but Takematsu thought up ways to make architecture transform the environment. He aimed to make architecture a filter to improve the environment while at the same time encouraging self-sufficiency. The firm makes a living creating many types of buildings including shops and residences.

A company called CIA planned the building. Their work embraces design strategy, branding, marketing, merchandise development, architectural planning and construction. Their director, Sy Chen, is known for his design of several trendy facilities in Tokyo. This project is one in a series conceived with the notion of 'retreat', which drew its inspiration from the lifestyle of hermits in Chinese philosophy. The firm made use of this concept elsewhere when designing dwellings and holiday homes. Hence, this building functions as a retreat within the metropolis, at the same time sheltering and revealing its occupants through its semi-translucent glass. It might be interpreted as a modern-day place of seclusion.

Above: **Trans Building Office and Gallery**.
Aluminium honeycomb glass, which has recently been attracting attention, covers the building in three directions

Above: **Trans Building Office and Gallery**. The rear of the building

Above left: **Trans Building Office and Gallery**.
Looking back at the far interior from the front of the third floor

Above right: **Trans Building Office and Gallery**.
Notice the protruding back of the fibre-reinforced plastic (FRP) kitchen unit/cupboard

Above left: Trans Building Office and Gallery.
The honeycomb pattern brings to mind a birdcage

Above right: Trans Building Office and Gallery.
The first floor houses a gallery. The step up to the
entrance is deliberately shallow

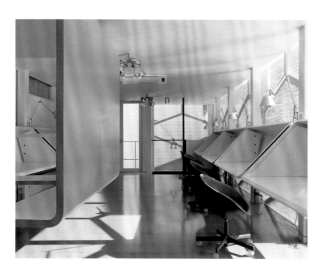

Above left: Trans Building Office and Gallery.
The third floor office

Above right: Trans Building Office and Gallery.
The third floor office is kept free of clutter

Above left: **Trans Building Office and Gallery**. The building is conceived as a retreat within the metropolis

Above right: **Trans Building Office and Gallery**. The designers used the ecologically friendly concept of 'Environment Altering Mechanism'

Above left: **Trans Building Office and Gallery**. One can see in the centre of the third floor office a partition unit attached to the ceiling to block off space for the president's use. The three faces of the unit can be used: the front face, the overhead space and the rear

Above right: **Trans Building Office and Gallery**. A stairway

Ogilvy & Mather Japan

Location: Shibuya-ku
Completion date: 2003

Masamichi Katayama

The atmosphere of advertising agency offices mixes the formal and informal in varying degrees. The speech and appearance of those in the creative departments seem casual while those in management positions appear more businesslike. People in jeans and sportswear pass by 'the suits' in the hallways, while creative types and social butterflies stand exchanging pleasantries. It looks like something one might see in a television studio. How to bring out the sparkling creativity needed to impress clients while incorporating a lightness not seen in other industries becomes the trick to designing offices for advertising agencies.

Above: **Ogilvy & Mather Japan**. A reception desk is situated in the centre of each floor

All the offices of Ogilvy & Mather Japan Group that used to be scattered across the Ebisu area were moved into a brand-new office on the 25th floor of a high-rise in Shibuya-ku. The company executives wanted to create a stimulating work environment suitable for an international advertising agency, an environment that would inspire ideas. They wanted to turn the offices into a fun place, combining the ambience of campus and art school, for, according to the company philosophy, education is an important part of their culture and will play an even more key role in the future of successful organisations. An executive at Ogilvy & Mather took a liking to the creativity and ideas described in a magazine piece focusing on Katayama. In turn his colleagues took an interest in Katayama, who had been making a splash in countries outside Japan with his innovative ideas. They contacted him and he entered the contest to design the space. He was able to provide spectacular answers to all the company's design requirements and the clients chose him: he helped them realise exactly the type of office they were hoping for.

An elevator hall forms the nucleus of the office and opens up to a symmetrical H-shaped form. As no other tall buildings stand in the vicinity, the office boasts an exquisite panoramic view of Tokyo. The double-surface window side is used as a common space, and when prep meetings are not being held here people use it as a free space. Taking advantage of the view has been a comparatively recent trend; in the past enjoying the view was a luxury savoured only by the bigwigs, while most employees sat in a large unpartitioned room. Their backs towards the windows, they toiled at their jobs.

The main workspace at OMJ appears to retain a bit of formality in the office in terms of layout and materials. This balances with the openness provided by the window side's common space so that people can let off steam and regain their efficiency.

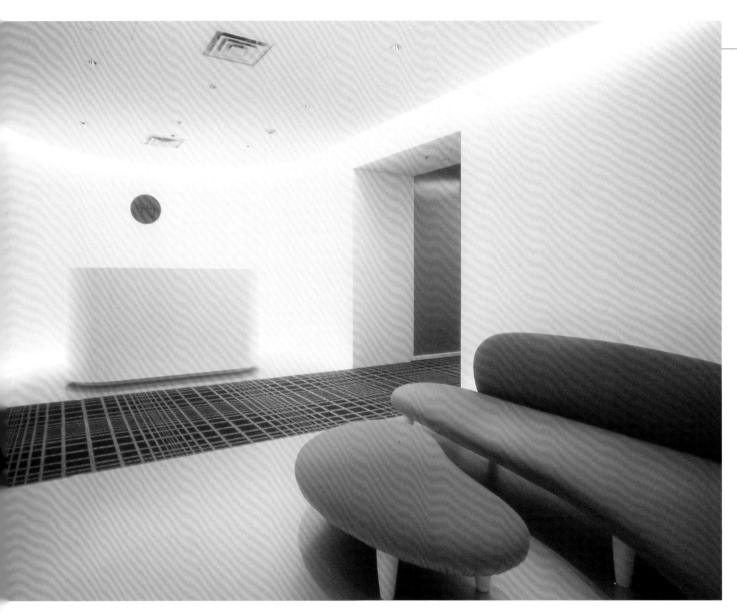

Above: Ogilvy & Mather Japan. The reception area. The red company logo mark stands out prominently in this white space. Chairs by Isamu Noguchi

Left: Ogilvy & Mather Japan. The carpet displays a simple motif that creates an unusual visual effect when one walks on it

Top left: **Ogilvy & Mather Japan**. The ample, long table provides the perfect setting for employees to brainstorm

Top right: **Ogilvy & Mather Japan**. The designers went out separately to furnish the offices with pieces that do not come together in a particular theme. They aimed to give the place the feel of an art school

Above: **Ogilvy & Mather Japan**. A passageway that divides two areas. The space is presently decorated with Kanji characters that express the ideals of the company

Bottom right: **Ogilvy & Mather Japan**. A floor with a great window view was set aside for employees to hold informal meetings or to take a break

Above: **Ogilvy & Mather Japan**. A room for informal meetings

Above: **Ogilvy & Mather Japan**. The conference room is a fine space for making presentations to clients

Right: **Ogilvy & Mather Japan**. The designers contrived to use a chandelier within this simple space to evoke a sense of lightness and merriment while lending just the right touch of tension

Sony Showroom &

Qualia Tokyo

Location: Ginza 5–3–1, Chuo-ku
Completion date: 2003

CURIOSITY – Gwenael Nicola + Reiko Miyamoto

Land prices in Ginza are the highest in Japan. In 1961, Sony decided to open a showroom at the most prominent spot on the intersection. They commissioned architect Yoshinobu Ashihara and invested an enormous sum in the building, which was completed in 1966 and took the spiral construction of New York's Guggenheim Museum as the inspiration for its structure. Having a large central pillar, each square floor splits into four divisions. There is a 90-centimetre gap between the floors and the building is constructed in such a way that by going through the place once you manage to skip an entire floor in space because of the incorporation of a spiral.

A small plaza that has become a famous spot in Tokyo was built facing the intersection. An entire wall of Sony-made TV monitors, which were the forerunners of today's large screens, ran along the street. The building gradually grew decrepit, and the surroundings changed a great deal with buildings such as the Renzo Piano-designed, glass-block Maison Hermès sprouting up in the vicinity of the Sony Building. In 2003, the showroom at the centre of the building was renovated.

French-born Gwenael Nicola was selected as the designer of this showroom. After studying interior design in Paris he went on to learn industrial design at the RCA in London. He set up Curiosity in Tokyo in 1999. The company participates in a broad spectrum of design ranging from perfume bottles, video game machines and vehicle navigation systems to stores, furniture and architectural projects.

Before winning the competition to design the showroom Nicola paid a visit to Sony and drank in the splendour of the old building. He took advantage of the pre-existing skip-floor construction to install a spiral glass wall that extends from top to bottom. At the same time he unified the previously disparate interior decor of each floor under a single theme. He thought up the concept of 'a tower within a building' which he felt expressed not only the merchandise but also the quintessence of Sony. He felt confident of winning the competition, and indeed his proposals scored a direct hit.

At the same time as he undertook the showroom refurbishment, Nicola also designed the first shop for the brand Qualia. These stores, which are directly managed by Sony, have become an important venue for meeting customers face-to-face. Aside from the Ginza store, Sony runs two other outlets, one in Tokyo's Odaiba and the other in Osaka's Shinsaibashi. Here, the showroom is done out in blue glass; to distinguish it from other areas the ceiling is black with a lustre reminiscent of a lacquer finish. The ceiling reflects light off the glass, suffusing the entire space with an extraordinary atmosphere.

Above: **Sony Showroom & Qualia Tokyo**. Second floor of the showroom. The details are transparent

Above: **Sony Showroom & Qualia Tokyo**. Booths for internet users are on the fifth floor

Right: **Sony Showroom & Qualia Tokyo**. The mid-floor area of the showroom between the second and third floors

Above: Sony Showroom & Qualia Tokyo.
Hanging displays for laptop computers

Left: Sony Showroom & Qualia Tokyo. One walks
along the glass wall as if going along a street and
perusing the merchandise. When one wants to
know more about the products one goes outside
the wall, realising the vision of an 'inside out' design

Above: **Sony Showroom & Qualia Tokyo**. The concept was to insert a blue column in the building, whose construction means that it skips a floor

Left: **Sony Showroom & Qualia Tokyo**. A view of the third floor display that brings the left-hand floor and ceiling together

Below: **Sony Showroom & Qualia Tokyo**. The Qualia shop on the fourth floor. The display shows off a Minimalist style

Above: **Sony Showroom & Qualia Tokyo**. A glass
wall divides each floor into two zones

Above: **Sony Showroom & Qualia Tokyo**. The
Qualia shop is the first store for Sony's new brand

Above: **Sony Showroom & Qualia Tokyo**. The
Qualia shop on the fourth floor. A consultation
counter sits on the left

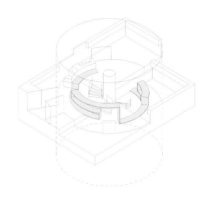

Above: **Sony Showroom & Qualia Tokyo**. Section

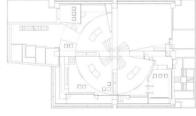

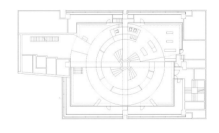

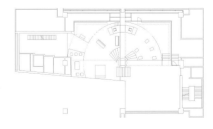

Above: **Sony Showroom & Qualia Tokyo**.
Floor plans

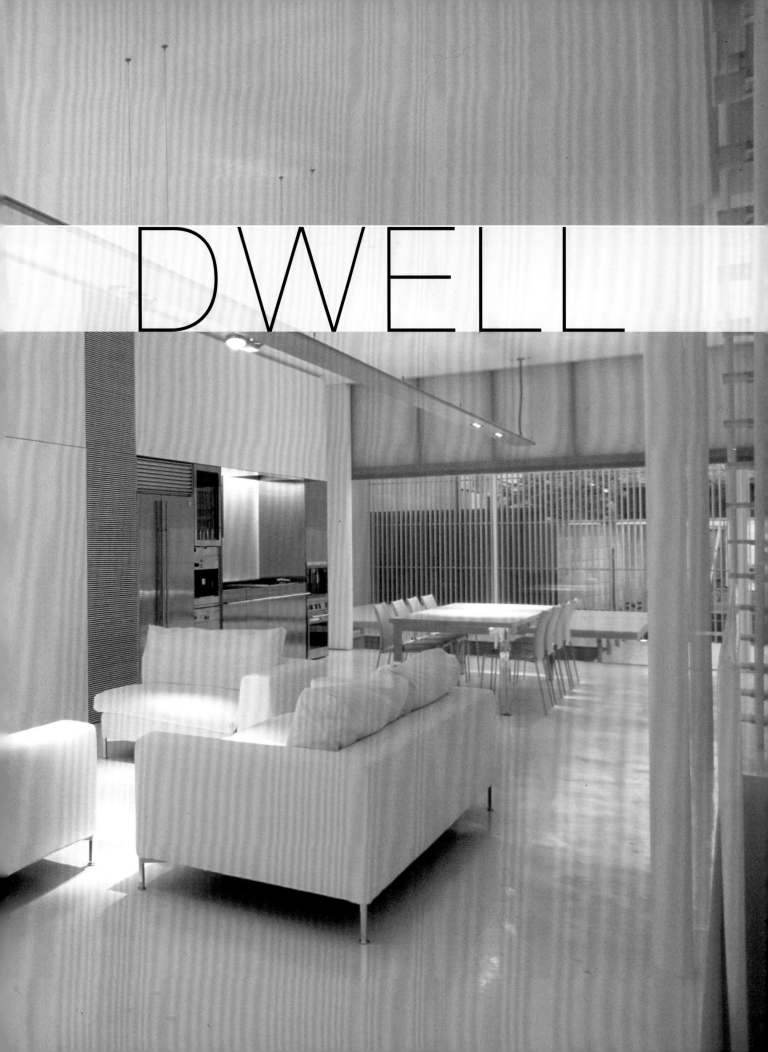

DWELL

In Japan people are increasingly building individual dwellings that overturn the hitherto conventional wisdom of shape and material. These places sprout up like mushrooms between buildings as well as in the somewhat chaotic high-density residential areas and nightlife districts. Especially in a place like Tokyo where there is minimal space available for detached dwellings, houses get built in spaces that people in other parts of the world would simply give up on. These include cramped premises where one side takes up only a few dozen centimetres and is bordered by sharp angles. Incredibly, on such seemingly unpromising premises architects have succeeded in crafting stylish residences, creating a boom in 'diminutive dwellings'. Tokyo's housing market has become something of a laboratory for experimenting with many types of revolutionary shapes and techniques in construction while using the cutting edge in materials such as glass, steel and fibre-reinforced plastic.

Tokyo differs from the world's other great cities in that it has many detached residences, while no other city offers such a high number of progressive individual dwellings. A variety of factors contributed to the background to the housing boom. With the relaxation of architectural

regulations people are allowed to fill vacant lots with houses. Also, the government encourages the building of residences, be they housing complexes or detached dwellings. Furthermore, due to inheritance tax laws it is better to retain even small properties and cling on to them (the Japanese are overly fixated on owning land). It is noteworthy, too, that the shrinking divide between architects and their clients has led to a growing trend in custom-built housing catering to the owner's preferences in design and lifestyle. It is a trend that gives added impetus to the re-evaluation of the conventional homogenised urban lifestyle.

After a period of modernisation in the 19th century, Japanese living in the cities were able to enjoy the freedom of owning their own homes, but they were poor at choosing and building those homes. Until recently, people regularly tended to purchase 'spec homes' or condominiums just as they were built by housing contractors. There tended to be little choice in layout, in many instances creating places ill-suited to modern living. Now people can at last follow their own tastes when choosing a house just as they would for cars, watches or clothes.

Traditionally speaking, the Japanese have a Buddhist-based world view that holds that the world as we know it is ephemeral and all things pass out of existence. In line with this philosophy, they had a propensity to view their dwellings as temporary, and cases in which families continue living in the same house over an extended period of one or two centuries, as is seen in Europe, are extremely rare.

Interest in dwellings and 'living' has now considerably increased. The younger generation in particular places great emphasis on living stylishly and certainly nowadays Japanese dwellings have become the personal 'castles' of the young people in which they can display their individual styles. It remains to be seen whether this trend will expand to become something that all generations can embrace comfortably.

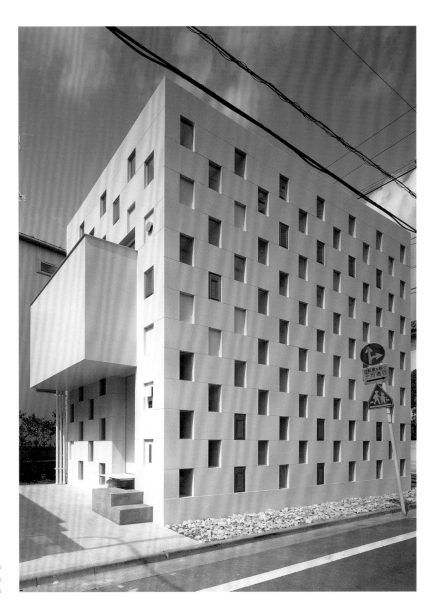

Right: **Cell Brick**. At first glance this looks as if it is built with concrete blocks, but the units are actually steel boxes

Natural Ellipse

Location: Shibuya-ku
Completion date: 2002

Masaki Endo

Left: Natural Ellipse. Light comes in through a window in the roof. Reinforced glass in the window is strong enough to walk on

The shape of this house surprises people when they first see it as it looks as though an enormous chrysalis has been erected. They receive another shock when they take in the fact that clients actually commissioned a residence like this – and found someone to realise their vision.

People who request Masaki Endo to build their residences often seek him out after being seduced by one of his experimental pieces. They generally have the desire to change their lifestyle to one that matches the lifestyle his dwellings present. The clients who commissioned him to design Natural Ellipse wanted to change their entire surrounding world when they built their home. They chose to build in an area of Shibuya that brims with youthful energy and is near many clubs and 'love hotels'. They ventured to buy the land with the intention not only of revitalising Tokyo architecture but also of surprising people with a house of such impact. Rather than conventionally requesting Endo to produce a specific design or number of rooms, the clients furnished him with detailed accounts of their daily lives from when they woke up until they went to bed, including such points as what they wore and what they ate. They wanted him to produce a design that would complement and support their lifestyles.

When planning this project Endo decided to adhere meticulously to the concept of the oval. He has a fondness for designing each portion piecemeal and then bringing these disparate elements together. At first glance this might look like a digitally contrived building, but Endo is not the type to assemble his designs by bringing together three-dimensional images on a computer monitor. Designing this house required working out precisely how to make the exterior come together with the interior. After repeatedly sketching arcs, he had the sudden brain wave to include everything within an oval.

Born in 1963, Endo independently set up Endo Design House in 1994. He has received numerous awards, and in 2003 the Japan Institute of Architects crowned him with the Newcomer's Award, an honour that often augurs considerable success for architects.

Above: Natural Ellipse. 24 long, narrow oval rings stand perpendicularly, seamlessly covered with fibre-reinforced plastic (FRP). The house sits in the dead centre of a bustling shopping and entertainment district in Shibuya

Right: Natural Ellipse. The building stands 10.8 metres tall. The outside wall uses heat-resistant FRP, coated with Gore-Tex (water-resistant paint)

Above: **Natural Ellipse**. Including the first level of the basement, the building has five levels with two families in residence

Above: **Natural Ellipse**. The spiral staircase cascades down to the study in the first level of the basement

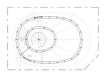

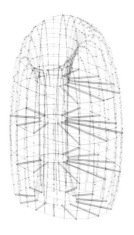

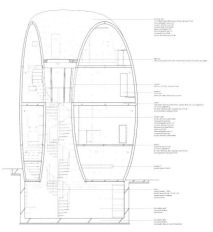

Above: **Natural Ellipse**. Floor plans

Left: **Natural Ellipse**. Essential facilities are organized around the circulation core

Above left: **Natural Ellipse**. Plan of the framework

Above right: **Natural Ellipse**. Section

Plastic House

Location: Meguro-ku
Completion date: 2002

Kengo Kuma

A famous essayist and her son, a former model turned would-be young photographer, reside in this house. Both have lived in a variety of cities abroad as well. In her lifetime the essayist has changed residences more than 40 times, experiencing everything from a grand estate to a 4½-tatami (straw mat) tenement. (Japanese real estate is often measured in traditional tatami space. One tatami is usually 1.82 metres x 92 centimetres.) Wanting to live somewhere with plenty of breathing space she once bought a house in Canada, but eventually she decided to live with her son in Tokyo.

They wanted to get away from the Japanese LDK (attached living room/dining room/kitchen) layout, but after searching in vain for a property that met their requirements, the clients decided to build their own home. By chance the future client and photographer met Kengo Kuma at a forum and duly asked him to build their house.

Kuma explained that he wanted to build a house in the heart of the city made out of plastic: 'a material in which the interior and exterior become one and bring out a soft environment.' This house became the realisation of this image, and the commission marked Kuma's first design for an ordinary dwelling. The photographer grew increasingly interested in the house and set about doing research on it himself. He actively participated in the process to the point where he and the designer had many heated discussions on the project.

At first, the clients wanted a columnless, completely plastic house constructed along the lines of Lego blocks, but they were forced to give up on this idea after the research costs ballooned and they found out that permission for this method of construction would take some time. As a result only portions of the interior and exterior of the elevations were made out of plastic while the rest of the house was produced using conventional methods and materials. They assembled 4-millimetre-thick plates of FRP (fibre-reinforced plastic) with various pipes for the framework to make the ceiling, floors and walls. They also made the stairs from FRP grating. In addition, in order to allow for more light to permeate the materials, they tried to use screws of see-through plastic wherever practicable. They gave consideration to translucency by not using aluminium batten, choosing instead caulking compound and isobutene-isoprene rubber (IIR) for the screws. Since all these materials transmit light easily the morning sunlight wakes the residents quite early. Natural light is complemented by the fact that the clients had most of the interior swathed in white – hence the photographer holds shoots in the house.

Above: **Plastic House**. The outside view of the front face on the west side

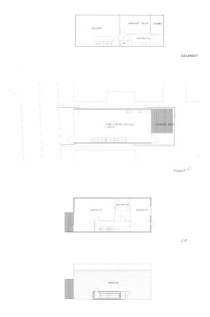

Above: **Plastic House**. Floor plans

Above: **Plastic House**. FRP blends the
translucency of plastic with a certain texture

Above: **Plastic House**. On top of the roof

Above: **Plastic House**. The walls on the first floor have been kept plain so this area can be used as the photographer's studio

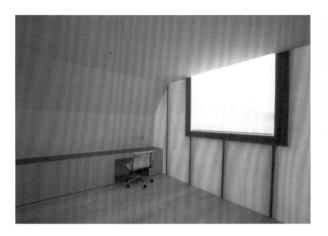

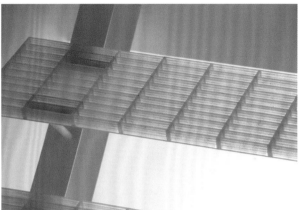

Above left: **Plastic House**. The walls of the east
bedroom on the second floor couple FRP panels
with insulation that blocks out light

Above right: **Plastic House**. Detail of the stairway

Above: **Plastic House**. The first floor serves as a
living room, dining room and kitchen

Above: **Plastic House**. The east side nightscape

Above: **Plastic House**. FRP louvres above the areaway, which can be used as a roofless tearoom

Right: **Plastic House**. The house is located in a tranquil area and has a park in front of it

Above: **Plastic House**. Kuma says of the house: 'We took advantage of the good parts of Tokyo, and this design fits right into the context of Tokyo.'

Natural Illuminance

Location: Edogawa-ku,
Completion date: 2001

Masaki Endo

In Japan's cities so-called 'mini-developments' have gained in popularity. A 'mini-development' means a small-scale structure which is on the site of less than 100 square metres (if the regulations set the standard at 300 square metres, then a space smaller than that) and is divided into residences for sale. Previously such a small space wouldn't have been the target of developers. Now, normal practice entails dividing what originally would have been about the space for one building into three parts and constructing three mini-developments on the site (mainly out of wood). From the standpoint of the scenery this is hardly welcome, but due to the relaxation of building regulations such developments have proliferated rapidly and as many houses as possible are crammed into the smallest spaces.

This mini-development lies in the corner of what used to be a field, which was divided into six portions to build houses. Other residences soon surrounded the Natural Illuminance house and the building put up next door obscured the striking south-side grid elevation. The owners of the house anticipated this obstacle to their greatest wish: to build a house that allowed lots of sunlight to enter.

Faced with such a challenge, Endo devised a method of collecting the heat insulation, natural illumination, vents and storage space in a single area. The building makes use of white square panelling to construct a vertically and horizontally uniform room that becomes a 'light box'. Black columns were assembled on the north side to function as building support. Light seeps in through the gaps between the panels and these units open individually allowing the space to get a good breeze. On the inside the wall units become storage space. With a ceiling height of 4 metres the building feels much more spacious inside than outside appearances would lead one to believe. Night or day, the illuminance of the room stays constant. The light that pours in through the panels during the day keeps the room just as bright as when the lights are turned on at night, making for an interior that enjoys the same amount of light whatever the time.

Above: Natural Illuminance. Three of the home's elevations are fitted with square panels. Each elevation has some panels that can either open or close

Above: Natural Illuminance. Just inside the entrance a 4-metre flight of stairs leads up to the second level

Above: **Natural Illuminance**. A young couple live in this home
with a living room on the first floor; in the future they will partition
off part of the space to make a child's room

Above: **Natural Illuminance**. The second floor
kitchen. The dining room and living room are on the
left-hand side

Above: **Natural Illuminance**. In the bedroom on
the first floor, the light that comes through the slit
glass is enchanting. The flooring is made of
polyvinyl chloride resin tiles

Above: **Natural Illuminance**. The exterior features neatly aligned 1.2 x 1.2 metre panels. The gaps between the perimeters of the squares have double-skin slits of glass and acrylic resin

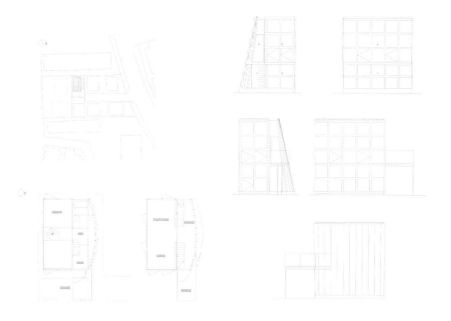

Above left: **Natural Illuminance**. Floor plans   Above right: **Natural Illuminance**. Elevations

Above: **Natural Illuminance**. The pillars on the north side help to support the entire structure

Drawer House

Location: Toshima-ku
Completion date: 2003

Oki Sato

From a distance the high cedar-board picket fence might look like a simple enclosure, but it conceals a concrete house situated behind it. The fence was put up in order to tone down the otherwise oppressive appearance that comes from exposing concrete. The building has doors on the upper portion of the north and south sides but no windows. All the functional elements, starting with furniture such as the shelf, bed and table, as well as the stairs and even working areas such as the kitchen, can be stored to the side of the house, and only when the occupants need them do they take them out from the wall. These storage units can also serve as room partitions. A bathtub is located on the second floor and since the tub sits on a railing, the owners can slide it outside from the bathroom to the wood terrace to enjoy an outdoor bath.

If you store everything on the first and second floors, the place looks like an empty tunnel. Since literally everything in the interior can be stored, architects call it a 'drawer house'. The man who put this place together, Oki Sato, was born in Canada when his father's job was transferred abroad. He lived there until high school, and while studying architecture at a Japanese university he set up his design company Asyl. Aside from architecture, he undertakes CI, graphic, interior and product design.

The young architect's father owns the Drawer House. The family had lived in rented accommodation, but decided to build a new home. They created a layout with an audio room for the father while the mother wanted adaptability to allow for the family to grow. One sister, who was studying photography, wanted a darkroom. The other sister wanted room for her Japanese-style painting (this takes up space since the paper is spread out on the floor). Sato spent three years conceiving a plan that would meet all their needs.

The premises were cramped and the space doesn't benefit from much sunlight, but Sato came up with a variety of devices and constructed his first dwelling on this plot. Architects over 50 usually take the city of Tokyo's disorderliness as a negative, but increasingly the younger generation of practitioners seem to work with this difficulty. Sato especially has a flexible way of thinking due to his experience living abroad. While the construction and design of this dwelling mark his debut as a house builder, he has already designed a French restaurant in a project that entailed completely wrapping the premises in white canvas on a site overlooking a stream in a disorderly part of town. This innovative building shines at night and reflects upon the water like a giant, glowing lantern.

Above: Drawer House. The house lies beyond the wooden plank enclosure

Above: Drawer House. The stairs down to the basement from the first floor. Downstairs the architect made a bedroom and audio room for his father

Right: **Drawer House**. View from inside the
enclosure

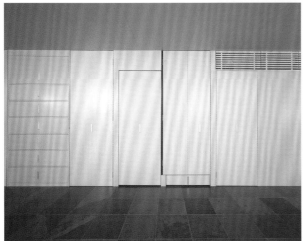

Above left: **Drawer House**. The pull-out furniture
on the first floor when it is closed up

Above right: **Drawer House**. The first floor furniture
when it is pulled out. The stairs also come out

Left: **Drawer House**. All elements except the dining table and chairs are hidden

Above: **Drawer House**. The first floor furniture has been pulled out in preparation for a meal

Right: **Drawer House**. The bed when it is pulled out, on the second floor

Above: **Drawer House**. The second floor bathtub is fixed to a rail so that it can be slid out for an outdoor bath

Above: **Drawer House**. The second floor with everything put away

Below: **Drawer House**. The bookshelf when it is pulled out, on the second floor

Above and below: **Drawer House**. Views towards
the second floor south-side terrace

Above: **Drawer House**. Floor plans

K House

Location: Nerima-ku
Completion date: 2003

Shinichi Ogawa

The clients who commissioned K House had lived abroad before and decided that if their requirements couldn't be met in Japan they would give up building a house there and simply live elsewhere. Japanese who have lived abroad often feel let down when they return home and are forced to deal with such things as the exorbitant price of housing (especially in the cities), the small size of houses, the insipid design and the difficulty in using the layout. In the end they usually accept the reality and learn to live with it. However, recently things have begun to change and it has become possible to have a place built by someone sympathetic to the client's personal taste.

A young couple with two children own K House and the wife spent a long time searching for architecture that was to her liking. She discovered Shinichi Ogawa's creations when reading an architecture magazine. However, the couple did not rush to request his services but took some time to think things through. Eventually, they were won over by Ogawa's understated aesthetic of which they felt they would never tire.

The characteristic quality of the homes Ogawa builds is a flawlessly smooth surface which produces a look like a Minimal box with no obtrusive features in sight. To achieve this the doors, window frames, electrical outlet board, air-conditioning unit and storage opener have all been mounted in as far as possible, or else fitted so they do not stand out. A devotee of Mies and Kahn, Ogawa made the third floor fireplace out of glass to look like a modern Japanese version of Miesian style. This place also serves as the focal point for the family's interaction.

In this house they can use the space freely, adjusting it to their changing lifestyles. Each room on the second floor has movable furniture and they can partition the space in whatever way they like. If they undo the holding sash on the third floor's south-facing terrace, they can extend the living room even further by incorporating the terrace as part of the living room.

Born in 1955, Ogawa honed his craft at New York's Architectronica and while working in Paul Rudolph's office. In 1986 he set up on his own, working out of his Hiroshima base.

Above: **K House**. The dining area

Above: K House. The walls are so smooth that it is hard to even
locate a light switch. The surface is ideal for projected images

Above left and right: K House. Simple and smooth
details in the bathroom

Above: **K House**. The stairway

Above: **K House**. A hallway

Above left and right: K House. The centre and side of the kitchen space

Above: K House. View of the dining area from inside the kitchen

Above and opposite: **K House**. The dining and living room

section A   section B

Above left: **K House**. Sections

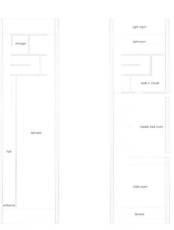

1st floor plan   2nd floor plan   3rd floor plan

Above right: **K House**. Floor plans

Cell Brick

Location: Suginami-ku
Completion date: 2004

Yasuhiro Yamashita

For large homes the thickness of the walls is not much of an issue, but in Tokyo's diminutive dwellings wall thickness is a perennial concern. Homes usually use about 15 centimetres of material for the exterior wall, but some builders have reduced this to 1/25th the normal size by using sheets of 6-millimetre-thick steel plates. Such techniques help to expand volume, and for people who live in such confining premises even that much of a change makes a big difference.

Yasuhiro Yamashita built Cell Brick as part of a series of abodes called 'skin wall houses' which reduce the floor slabs and exterior walls to wafer-thin levels in order to avoid infringing the various municipal regulations governing construction on small lots. Yamashita comments: 'We are probably the only ones to erect homes with 6–9 millimetre thick steel exteriors. The existence of slim layer houses seems so very characteristic of Tokyo architecture.' Born in 1960, he set up the architectural firm Yamashita Kai Architectural Lab in 1991, when he was 31. Yamashita renamed the studio Atelier Tekuto in 1997. One after another he has produced unique residences that are high in design-sense while super-low in cost. He takes part in projects to make architect-fashioned, functional houses that can also accommodate those on tighter budgets.

Here he constructs the exterior by alternately piling up 450 x 900 x 300 millimetre steel storage boxes, a size that adheres to traditional Japanese measurements. By adding a touch of masonry to the mix the builders came up with a house-building method that uses a technique of heaping up metal units. The box units shut out the summer sunlight while taking in the winter light. The inside and outside became more practical with the application of NASA-developed insulating paint, which has been used before in other residences.

In the case of this house, at the first preparatory meeting the clients made only three main requests: a place that did not need curtains; a place they did not need to buy furniture for; and a place with an interior that cannot be imagined by viewing the outside. In the process of the ongoing discussions the clients came up with some novel ideas such as siting the washing machine above the toilet and placing the bathtub in a space that makes it appear to float. Yamashita gives credit to them for half the ideas for this structure.

Cell Brick sits on the corner of a tranquil residential area, and the female client in her 50s, who helped in the design process, lives here with her son and daughter who are in their 20s. While Tokyo undoubtedly stands out among the world's cities in terms of design for eating and drinking establishments as well as shops, this creativity has spread to the design of residences as well. Tokyo's small lots need not necessarily be considered a disadvantage since the size has become a catalyst for improvement in technology and the pursuit of function, construction and design. It is precisely because this is Tokyo that architects have many opportunities to experiment in this way.

Above: **Cell Brick**. In order to fully utilise the lot, the architect worked out how to make a house from thin steel board

Above: **Cell Brick**. Since the building sits on a corner lot, some passers-by do not realise that it is a dwelling

Below: **Cell Brick**. The client conceived the idea of making the bathtub appear to float in mid-air

Above: **Cell Brick**. The steel box (450 x 900 x 300 millimetres) fits Japan's traditional architectural units of measurement

Above: **Cell Brick**. The basement contrasts with the above-ground levels as it is very normal

Above: **Cell Brick**. Looking down from the second floor. The owner is an artistic woman who wanted a house that had some panache

Above: **Cell Brick**. The washing machine is in the middle of the spiral stairway

Above: **Cell Brick**. The boxes help storage

Right: **Cell Brick**. Stacked-up boxes make a chequered pattern

Above: **Cell Brick**. The builders chose to replace masonry with a system of house building that involved piling up metal units

Right: **Cell Brick**. At night the building looks spectacular with light pouring through the square openings

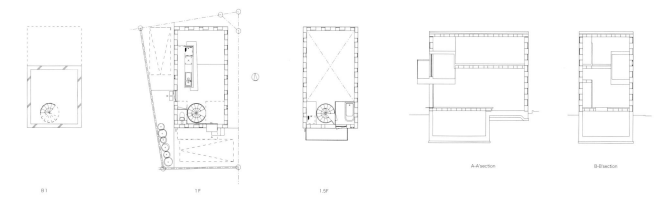

B1   1F   1.5F   A-A'section   B-B'section

Above: **Cell Brick**. Floor plans and sections

SAK

Location: Itabashi-ku
Completion date: 2001

Toshiaki Ishida

Surrounded by shops, pubs, video arcades and pachinko parlours, SAK faces a less than 3-metre squalid alley off the roadside. The silver walls are reminiscent of a giant samurai sword. The area is 16.4 metres in length, while the width goes from 3.5 metres at its widest to 2 metres at its narrowest. The owner of this store, which deals in second-hand clothes and goods, lives and does business in SAK. Born in 1950, Toshiaki Ishida built the place himself. He gained experience at the Toyoo Ito office and went on to become an award-winning designer who is numbered among modern Japan's foremost architects.

The neighbourhood's buildings are reflected in the dwelling's polished stainless-steel surface. Depending on the angle from which they are viewed and the direction of the light, the things reflected constantly shift: at times they appear smaller or larger, or merge completely into the background.

When looked at from outside, the building gives the impression of being completely closed off. The first floor houses the store, and from the inside it seems spacious since the entire surface features a 16-metre sliding door. In fact, the inside is so narrow that merely by stretching out one's arms one can touch both walls, but it was made intentionally narrow. On the third floor as one goes back into the interior the slant of the walls increases sharply, and the height of the ceiling changes from 1.6 metres to 4 metres. In this one dwelling it is possible to experience a variety of different spaces. The wood-wool cement boards applied to the interior walls look like hardened spaghetti. Architects make use of these boards, which combine cement with string-like strands of fine wood shavings, on roofs and the exterior walls of basements. This lightweight material has many benefits: it is easy to process, is flame resistant, acts as a sound barrier, absorbs sounds and provides excellent insulation. In the past, builders have often used it to back the roofs of school gymnasiums, but in recent years they frequently use it in residences as well. Ishida utilised wood-wool cement boards as he thought simply painting the walls white would be banal. From close up the pattern is visible and the texture is rough to the touch. The material lends the home a human feel while also being unusual. The house has a pronounced character and exudes a warmth created by casting aside Modernism.

When taking a look at the numerous unique houses that sprout up around Tokyo, it is noticeable that many of them seem quite eccentric – hence critiquing them from a traditional vision of housing becomes meaningless. Conversely, by observing and learning about these avant-garde homes one acquires a greater sense of how the things people seek in housing have changed, as well as how the concept of residences in general is changing in tune with the times.

Above: **SAK**. Located near a train station, SAK lines up parallel to the train tracks and makes quite an impression when seen from a train

Above: **SAK**. The house is situated in a commercial area with drinking establishments and a pachinko parlour

Above left: SAK. The owner of the house uses the first floor to run a store for second-hand clothing and goods

Above right: SAK. The surrounding scenery is reflected by the mirror facade of stainless steel, which helps to camouflage the presence of the house

Left: SAK. The south-side exterior. The area that looks like a rectangular hole is the terrace

Above: **SAK**. At its narrowest SAK is only about 2.6 metres wide

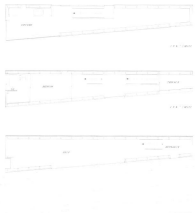

Above: **SAK**. Looking at the south side from the inside of the glass door on the second floor

Above: **SAK**. Floor plans

Above: **SAK**. The kitchen on the north side of the third floor. The horizontal hood, lying down at an angle of 90 degrees, was originally designed to hide the presence of the fans

Above left: **SAK**. The stairway between the second and third floors. If one proceeds to the far interior of the third floor the angle becomes sharp and the height of the ceiling rises from 1.6 to 4 metres

Above right: **SAK**. Rather than clichéd, bare concrete walls in the interior, wood-wool cement boards have been used. The texture has a warmth to it

Above left: **SAK**. The north side on the second floor.
The bedroom is far beyond the glass while the bath-
and restroom is even further back

Above right: **SAK**. The bare concrete wall meets
the wood-wool cement boards

When was the last time you truly had a chance to relax, and what kind of time was that? People have a lot of ways to unwind including family get-togethers, gatherings among friends, taking care of pets or immersing themselves in their hobbies.

In the changing business climate that followed hard on the collapse of the Bubble Economy, many Japanese felt mentally and physically drained and began to prioritise the place of relaxation in their lives. As if relaxation wasn't enough, the word *iyashi*, meaning 'healing', became a buzzword often tossed about by the mass media.

Iyashi can denote a variety of things encompassing such seemingly disparate sources of relaxation as hot springs, restaurants, bars, music and films. From the recent boom in *iyashi* it is clear that for the Japanese the forms of leisure have changed. For example, leisure for the businessmen of yesteryear meant golf, mahjong and karaoke – group activities that could be

enjoyed with business associates. However, many of the golf courses the corporate set depended on went bust during the recession, while mahjong lost popularity due to its smokey and unhealthy settings. At the same time karaoke establishments began a cut-throat price war.

Said to be a 10 billion yen-a-year business, only pachinko maintained its firmly rooted popularity despite the economic downturn (pachinko is a game played on what looks like a small pinball machine that is electrically operated and stands vertically). In common with PC games, playing pachinko is a solitary activity. When it comes to *iyashi*, this is also about the individual rather than the group. If one wishes to give it a positive slant one might say that solitary activities provide a rare opportunity for reflection; viewed negatively, these same activities can become unhealthy and even lead to antisocial behaviour.

Many choose to let off steam to the beat of music at discos, clubs, lounges and concerts. One could interpret the popularity of these venues as being part of a worldwide phenomenon. With the influence of globalism, similar music is played in all the developed capitalist countries and by association much music-related merchandise is in circulation. The cutting edge of this music culture always reaches Tokyo. However, since there remain clear cultural and linguistic differences, particularly between Japan and the Western economies, the same music isn't necessarily transmitted and absorbed in the same way. Essentially, what comes across is melody and rhythm; rhythm is particularly important as the urban cultures of capitalist countries synchronise themselves to this rhythm, so helping music create the shape of an invisible interior.

Below: **FIORIA aria blu**. A hallway in the karaoke dining bar

Baisouin Temple

Location: Minami-aoyama 2–26–38, Minato-ku
Completion date: 2003

Kengo Kuma

Even the bustling city contains old buildings and quiet parks suitable for relaxation. The shogunate commenced in 1603 and later, when the government shifted back to the emperor, they still called the city Edo even after the name had been changed to Tokyo. Vestiges of the old Edo can still be found here and there throughout the city, mostly in the form of temples and shrines. Even in this city that repeatedly scraps and rebuilds things, the shrines and temples demonstrate that Tokyo actually has a historical legacy.

Starting with Prada's glass-encased building, Aoyama has many spots that make it a Mecca for the style-conscious. Here Baisouin Temple was first built in 1643 as a memorial to Yukinari Aoyama, a samurai warrior who had seen long service with Ieyasu Tokugawa, the first of the Tokugawa shoguns. The place-name Aoyama derives from the fact that this family lived in the area. Earlier this temple had vast premises and stood as the nucleus of Aoyama. Aerial bombardment during the Second World War destroyed those portions of the temple that had been built in the Edo Period, and afterwards it was rebuilt several times. The pavilion erected in 1925 conformed to that era's wave of Modernism, merging Eastern and Western styles to produce a temple of steel-reinforced concrete. The building became dilapidated and was torn down in 2001. Kengo Kuma translated the temple into modern design language. Its present bamboo-framed approach is situated at the side of a large glass-walled building housing a computer service company that faces the avenue, Aoyama Dori. Most of those who work in Aoyama remain sublimely unaware that in the city's very heart there exists such a serene graveyard and events hall, with a basement and floors that seem to levitate on water.

In order to realise a programme intended to make Baisouin stand as a cultural centre in Aoyama, Kuma says he purposefully made use of neutral and abstract styles. He points out that the overt presence of religion has waned in Japan's cities, especially Tokyo. To grab the attention of those style aficionados who converge on the area he tried to depart from the traditional temple style as much as possible.

The horizontal parts of the roof extend down to the ground as if flowing off the roof, becoming louvres in the process. They create a buffer zone by integrating the foyer with the road, and at night-time the light from the building's interior is visible from Aoyama Dori, fusing the place with the surrounding environment. In building Baisouin the concept of a design open to the street was kept firmly in mind, while measures were taken to preserve the architecture from potential criminal damage in this urban setting. The architect also saw the possibilities inherent in creating an arresting low-level structure among high-rise buildings.

As a baptised Catholic Kuma has said that he would like to construct his own Catholic church, just as Le Corbusier made his ecclesiastic masterpiece Notre Dame du Haut. Kisho Kurokawa, one of modern Japan's foremost architects, purchased the cemetery and moved graves there from a temple in Nagoya.

Above: **Baisouin Temple**. The reception room

Above: **Baisouin Temple**. The fanlight in the old
temple pavilion has been recycled for use within
the new design

Above left: **Baisouin Temple**. The reception-room terrace area can hold shallow water, making it look as if the floor is floating

Above right: **Baisouin Temple**. The bamboo-surrounded entrance is reminiscent of a high-class, traditional Japanese restaurant. Glass-encased office buildings near the entrance make it unimaginable that it leads to a temple

Above: **Baisouin Temple**. The interior provides a space that the people in the area can use for a variety of events

Above: **Baisouin Temple**. The front side entrance. The open area in
front of the entrance is used for traditional dances. The main hall rests at
the top of the stairs

Right: **Baisouin Temple**. Floor plans

Above: **Baisouin Temple**. The main sanctuary as seen from the cemetery side. The high-rise buildings in the background are a housing complex

Right: **Baisouin Temple**. The entrance off Aoyama Dori connects to a hall that pays homage to Hounen, the founder of the Pureland (Joudo) Sect of Buddhism in Japan

Above: **Baisouin Temple**. The view from the reception room is a reminder that the temple lies at the heart of a megalopolis

Lounge NEO

Location: Dogenzaka 2–21–7, Shibuya-ku
Completion date: 2002

Haruo Taguchi

Designers are noted as a group who always adhere to their own particular tastes. These might include preferences for materials, colours, lighting or things that go beyond vision and have their resonance in the realms of thought and poetic consciousness. One of the things that project designer Haruo Taguchi had in mind for this space was an impressive wall that greets you as soon as you leave the elevator. Here he used a coated resin panel imported from America that sells under the product name Fish Eyes. Taguchi was strongly attracted to the material after seeing a magazine article about how Fish Eyes was used in the construction of the home pool for Lenny Kravitz's residence. He continued to wait for an opportunity to make use of the material, and says he was finally able to incorporate it in this project. A talent for discrimination is the very strength of a designer. As one of the most prolific and popular designers in the Kansai region, the Osaka-based young designer works out of the Tokyo office of Yoshihiko Mamiya's company, Infix.

This lounge occupies the sixth and seventh floors of a building in the Maruyama-cho district of Shibuya, an area situated near Bunkamura, an up-market cultural complex five minutes from Shibuya station. The structure was erected in 1989 under the guidance of Jean-Michel Wilmotte. However, Maruyama-cho used to be a red-light district and even today there remain many 'love hotels' that specifically target couples. After 1990 many concert venues and clubs sprang up around here and some dozen of these are concentrated along a 50-metre street. This is an unusually happening place for Japan and makes Maruyama-cho one of the centres of Shibuya youth culture.

In the same building there are four different clubs, all managed by the same company responsible for NEO: Vuenos, Club Asia P, Club Asia and Lounge NEO. It is mostly 18–25 year-olds who come to the other three venues which between them attract around 300,000 revellers every year. Building on its achievements and experience the company created NEO, targeting a crowd that ranges in age up to the 50s. NEO caters to the demand of older people who want a music-filled space in which to relax and let off steam late into the night but no longer have the energy to boogie until dawn. The adults who come to NEO have to wade through crowds of young people, but this is actually the intentional. The design conjures up nostalgia for disco, and disco parties are often held here.

Above: Lounge NEO. The passageway by the elevator. The wall decorations make a striking impression

Right: Lounge NEO. A DJ booth is in the middle, to the immedieate left of the doorway

Above: **Lounge NEO**. The bar by the entrance

Above: **Lounge NEO**. A bar below the sixth floor seating

Below: **Lounge NEO**. The mirror balls put customers in the mood to disco

Above: **Lounge NEO**. A lounge that targets adults

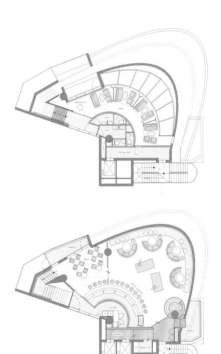

Above: **Lounge NEO**. Floor plans

Left: **Lounge NEO**. The view of the sixth floor
seating from the middle of the stairs

Left: **Lounge NEO**. Looking down from the sixth floor seating

Below: **Lounge NEO**. Images are dynamically projected on to the background on the sixth floor

Right: **Lounge NEO**. This circular floor uses the pre-existing floor construction

FIORIA aria blu, Tokyo

Location: Roppongi 5–1–3, Minato-ku
Completion date: 2003

Tsutomu Kobayashi

People think of Japan as the home of karaoke, which now enjoys worldwide popularity, while in Japan the business presently grosses billions of yen. Even if the market has levelled off, it is moving towards becoming a mature industry. In response to a business that calls for ever more upscale and diverse establishments, design has become a big factor in differentiating the market. The karaoke dining bar featured here is an example of a new trend in upscale karaoke venues.

The people who come here don't necessarily have to sing karaoke. The high performance, multifunctional karaoke machines are concealed in inconspicuous places and the space can be used for parties, dining, meetings or business consultations. Each of the 25 rooms flaunts a different design scheme. They include a banqueting hall with a seating capacity of 60, a reception room, a room prepared with costumes, one that echoes if a wall-affixed sensor is activated, a room with a lunar theme, and one with running hot water and a jacuzzi in which people can either immerse themselves or simply dangle their legs (this room comes equipped with bathing suits).

The VIP room requires IC cards (Integrated Circuit smart cards) to gain entry and can accommodate celebrities. Since the rooms have small, narrow windows privacy is not total, although they offer protection from the curious gaze of people outside.

When it comes to drinks and refreshments, until now karaoke rooms at best served pizza or spaghetti, but here one can order from a full menu complemented by a bar offering a wide variety of alcoholic beverages. In keeping with Roppongi's superior cachet, there is an extensive selection of wines and champagnes on offer.

The establishment is near the Roppongi intersection, the nucleus of the area. It occupies the third and fourth floors of a building that houses a classy flower shop that would not look out of place on New York's Fifth Avenue on the lower levels. A stairwell joins the two floors and the interior has the carefully contrived ambience of an Italian sidewalk.

Karaoke made its debut, mostly in drinking establishments, in the 1970s and originally drew an older crowd who came to sing traditional-style ballads known as *enka*. Once cable-transmitted karaoke was introduced, karaoke became a crucial market for the Japanese music industry. Whether or not ordinary people can comfortably sing a pop song has become a vital key to manufacturing a hit. IT now aids in the evolution of karaoke, which can mix with other forms of music, creating new types of business opportunities.

Above: **FIORIA aria blu**. Near the centre of the establishment is a passageway based upon those in Italian cities

Above: **FIORIA aria blu**. An overview of the open
space seen from the stairs

Above: **FIORIA aria blu**. The reception area looks like one in a hotel

Below: **FIORIA aria blu**. The room entitled 'FIORIA's Palace' is geared towards parties and can hold up to 60 people

Above: **FIORIA aria blu**. Floor plans

Left: **FIORIA aria blu**. The 'Sierra Saloon'. Lukewarm water flows through the room making it a fit place for a footbath

Above left: **FIORIA aria blu**. In the 'Spa Saloon' customers can wash or relax in the jacuzzi

Above right: **FIORIA aria blu**. Become one of the movers and shakers here in the 'Executive Saloon'. Customers must use IC cards to enter it, and the room feels like an executive lounge. People also use this space for business meetings

Below: **FIORIA aria blu**. The 'Juggler Saloon' features many holes in the wall. These contain sensors that respond with a variety of sounds when a hand is placed inside them

Above: **FIORIA aria blu**. Living up to its name, the 'Mirage Saloon' plays with people's vision as its floor and ceiling look like mirror reflections of each other

Left: FIORIA aria blu. Here in the traditional Western-style decor of the 'Masquerade Saloon' customers can enjoy dressing up in a variety of wigs and costumes

Right: FIORIA aria blu. FIORIA collaborated with Avex to create the 'Rave Room'. Avex is a major record company that grew rapidly due to the demand for dance music. The company's music videos can be enjoyed on the high performance audiovisual equipment

Below: FIORIA aria blu. The 'Luna Saloon' features an astral, sci-fi ambience. It is conceived as a hangar for UFOs on a planet

Avalon

Location: Dogenzaka 1–17–9, Shibuya-ku
Completion date: 2003

Katsunori Suzuki

In Tokyo, discos have made a comeback in popularity. Many of the legendary ones that got people jamming in the 1980s have one after another re-emerged. In the face of dwindling sales in the music industry, disco stands as an exception and compilation albums of yesterday's hits fly off the shelves in the tens of thousands. This is not limited to dance music – 1980s music as a whole has shown an increased profile and the world of fashion continues to switch gears from 1970s revival to 1980s revival.

Although the clubs that the younger generation revel in have reached saturation point, there were few places where adults could relax without worrying about dress codes and age, and their wishes have provided the stimulus for the rising demand in discos. Avalon doesn't simply focus on people in their 40s who went through disco the first time around; it also aims to attract younger people, allowing entry to men over 25 and women over 20. Avalon integrates the disco with dining – authentic European-style cuisine is served and vintage champagne is stocked. The DJ booth perches on the side of the dance floor and the layout includes a dining area seating 73 people, bar counter, VIP room and a dance stage (called an *otachidai*). A smoke machine stands ready, while on the ceiling a mirror ball and chandelier sparkle. The interior evokes disco of the 1970s and 1980s while the designers have consciously tried to temper some of the gaudier elements, for example replacing ones that would have been gold with silver ones. They filtered the interior, using today's tastes, with simple yet subtly detailed decorations to create a finished product with a sense of depth.

The stagnant economic conditions have continued for a long time and Japanese yearn for a taste of the gorgeous things and times that reached their peak in the 1980s (however, the quality of the extravagance, as seen in the Bubble era, has changed). Regardless of age, people who are fed up with the monotony of techno and hip-hop, or who simply can't keep up with them, can enjoy the 1980s music with its keen appreciation of the beauty of melody. It undoubtedly sounds refreshing. The design reflects this, as people who have had enough of Minimalism now crave a bit of outrageousness and flashiness. We have reached a point where even in a business context customers expect narrative marketing rather than direct marketing.

Above: Avalon. The demand for discos that adults can enjoy without worrying about age or dress codes has been increasing

Above: Avalon. Men under 25 and women under 20 are not allowed through the entrance

Right: Avalon. A VIP area geared towards women. Even the design of this establishment's powder rooms is ornate and fabulous

Above: **Avalon**. The VIP room shows off a revival of the sumptuous styles of the 1980s Bubble era

Below: **Avalon**. The executive lounge. People in their 40s and 50s can enjoy this space

Above: Avalon. The reception counter/cashier.
Since the sponsor of Avalon is a clothing brand, the
dresses in the background are its products. Here it
advertises and sells its wares, and all the female
staff members wear the brand's dresses

Above: **Avalon**. Floor plan

Right: Avalon. The toned down bar seems just
right for an adult-oriented lounge

Above: **Avalon**. The dance area is in the middle of the establishment. It lacks some of the flashiness of the Bubble days, but people still know how to party

Above: **Avalon**. As Avalon fuses a disco with a restaurant it serves authentic European cuisine, and even stocks vintage champagne

Left: **Avalon**. The club is trying to attract middle-aged people who would rather take it easy in a music-filled environment than relieve stress by boogieing down

Above: **Avalon**. Up to 73 people can sit in the dining area

Above: **Avalon**. People who are sick of social and economic stagnation want to savour a taste of the sublime days of the Bubble era

Mars the Salon

Location: Minami-aoyama 6–4–6, Minato-ku
Completion date: 2003

CURIOSITY – Gwenael Nicola + Reiko Miyamoto

Beauty salons for men have become more commonplace, but until recently shops would turn them down the moment they tried to make an appointment. The reason for this lay in the fact that women didn't care to have their makeovers done next to men (particularly in cases where there were no individual rooms). This up-market nail salon has individual rooms that offer pedicures and manicures to the upper crust. Men make up 40 per cent of the clientele with people in their 40s in the majority, but ages range from clients in their late 20s to those in their 70s. Customers include people running businesses in the area as well as doctors and even monks. The whole shop is arranged as individual 'treatment' rooms, and considerable care has been taken to avoid making it appear too girly by eschewing feminine interior design and keeping the decor simple so that men don't feel uncomfortable. Mars is situated in a two-storey building near the Aoyama jazz club, the Blue Note. A wooden deck stands by a terrace that faces a grove of trees next to an adjacent museum, and since the space below this is illuminated it feels as though the salon is above a pool. Both the floors of the individual rooms and the deck of the terrace are made of teak, eliminating unevenness while visually connecting the terrace with the rooms and conferring a sense of spaciousness.

Moreover, since the height of the individual rooms and size of the various areas are different, the rooms do not look the same. Gwenael Nicola took on the design of this space putting into practice an attention to detail that he learnt from Kyoto's Katsura Rikyu. At Katsura the placement of the buildings is set – and the particular size of each section of a building determined – by considering the onlooker's viewpoint. The several levels have been carefully laid out and while at first glance Katsura appears simple, actually it is heavy with many design devices that might be interpreted as alluding to Japanese architecture. In the salon, the store staff lead you inside to an interior filled with white light and a magical atmosphere that envelops people who cone into it.

Nicola also made all the original furniture, and the sofas are more comfortable than first-class seats on an aeroplane.

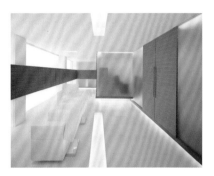

Above: Mars the Salon. The interior gives a nod to the style of Katsura Rikyu

Right: Mars the Salon. The designer assimilated and reinterpreted traditional Japanese architectural construction

Above: Mars the Salon. The door to the establishment is on the second floor of a modern, two-storey, concrete building

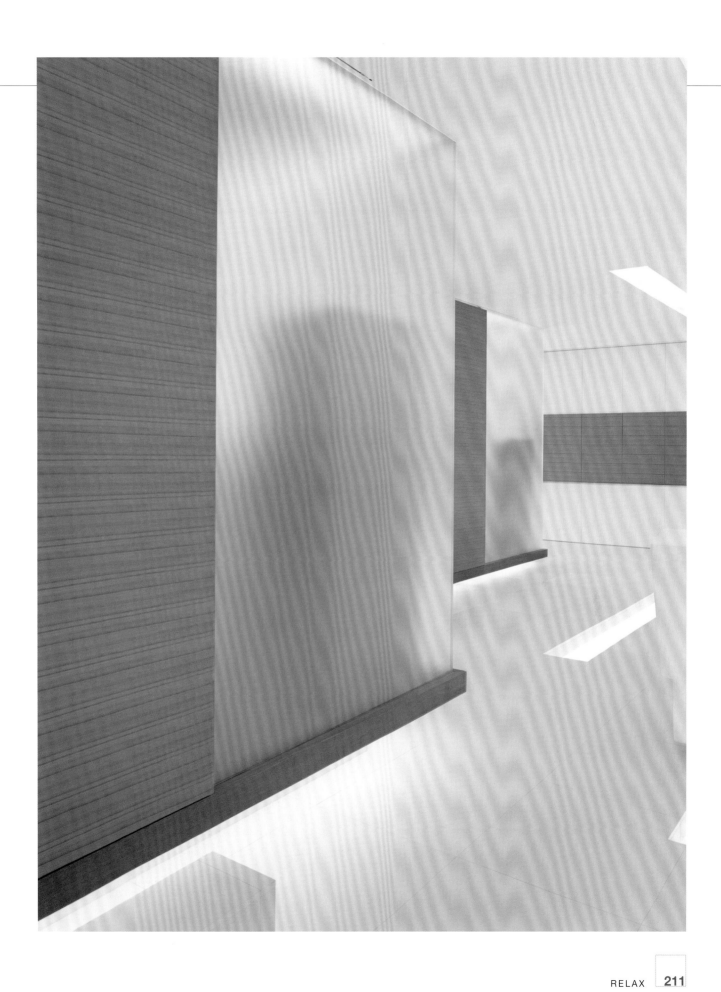

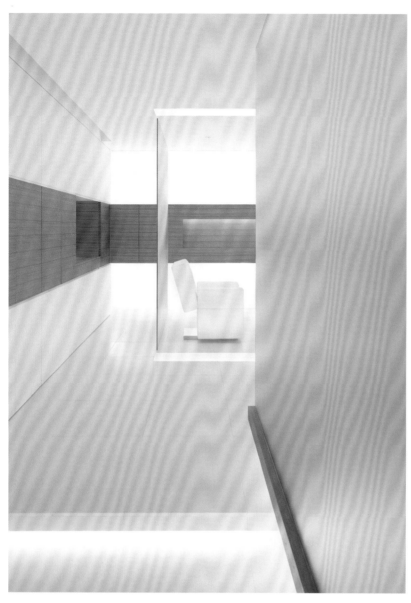

Top left: **Mars the Salon**. The place overflows with a refreshing feeling and a quietude stemming from the materials and colours used

Bottom far left: **Mars the Salon**. Starting with the sofa, all the furniture and knickknacks are the designer's original creations

Bottom near left: **Mars the Salon**. The sofas can open up to 180 degrees (horizontally) for the convenience of beauticians performing procedures on people's feet

Above left: **Mars the Salon**. The bamboo arranged in the vases by the entrance changes gradually from green to a whitish colour, adding a refined and austere touch to the place

Above right: **Mars the Salon**. There are intentionally many steps in the interior. The white cuboid blocks in the individual rooms conjure up images of the stones for one's shoes on the verandas of Japanese houses

Above: **Mars the Salon**. On the terrace side a grove of trees near the museum is visible, which helps to enhance the relaxing atmosphere

Right: **Mars the Salon**. The indirect lighting on the terrace's wooden decks creates the illusion of a pool of water

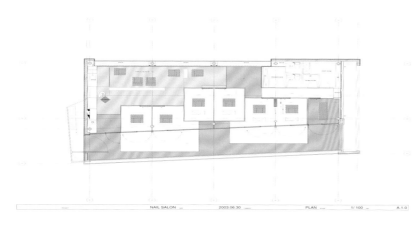

Above: **Mars the Salon**. Floor plan

TOKYO

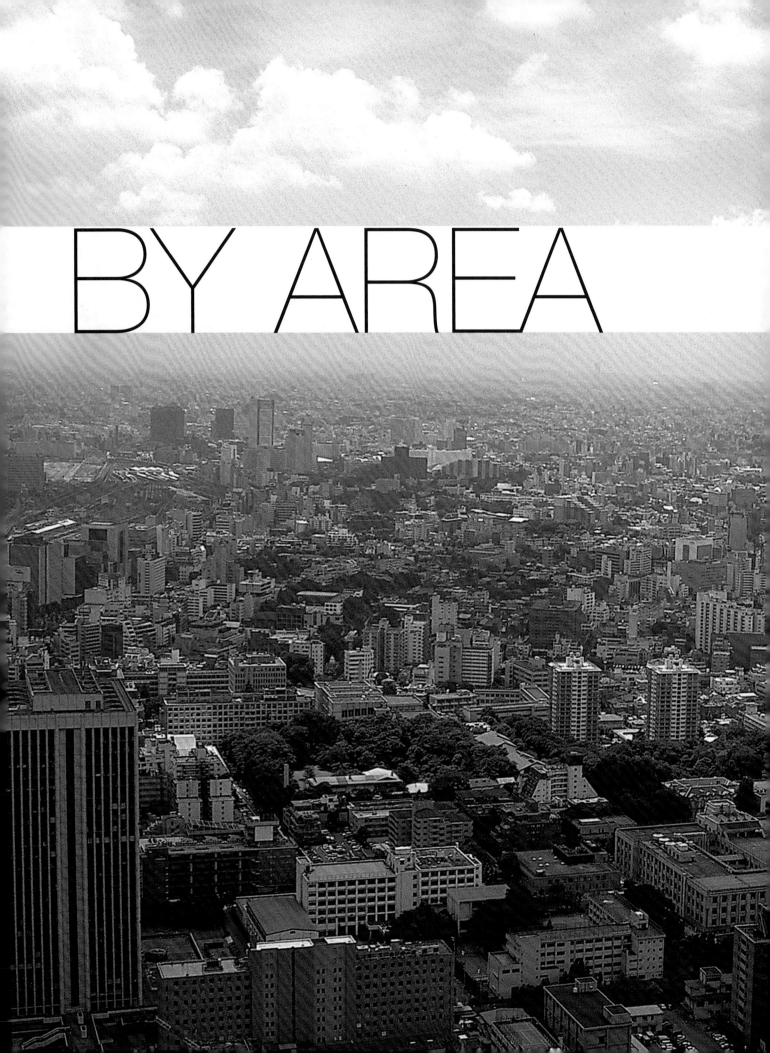

BY AREA

Tokyo by Area

The 23 Wards

The city of Tokyo is divided into 23 special administrative districts known as wards (*ku*) which make up the Tokyo Metropolitan Area. Several cities exist outside the special wards within the Metropolitan Prefecture of Tokyo, and many people are unaware that the topography of Tokyo's outlying areas to the west includes forests, mountains and deep valleys. People consider the region within the Yamanote Loop (Train) Line the core of Tokyo, a space that covers about the same area as Manhattan. Prior to the Second World War this interior area flourished as the commercial and entertainment hub, but afterwards development around the stations which dot the upper area of the Yamanote Line accelerated. Development began to extend out from stations such as Shinjuku, Shibuya, Harajuku, Ebisu and Shinagawa, and much of the city's culture followed suit with a trend emerging for development at the peripheries. Here we will take a brief look at those places which have become fashionable over recent years as well as places that have flourished due to redevelopment.

Shinjuku

Shinjuku accommodates a huge variety of things with each area displaying completely different features. Many bus and train lines converge at Shinjuku station with about three million people using it each day. To the east and west sides of the station are located many department stores and fashionable commercial buildings, and between these a plethora of large and small shops, restaurants, karaoke pubs and pachinko parlours operates. Gaudy neon, a superabundance of signs, noisy recorded announcements and sound effects from video arcades all add to the din, making it so noisy that sometimes one can't even hear oneself think. An area known as Kabuki-cho has a red-light district resembling that of a Southeast Asian country, and within its recesses Asians and Latin Americans go about their business. Down the street from Kabuki-cho in an area called '2 Chome', dozens of bars and clubs cater to Tokyo's increasingly visible gay community. At the same time the western side of the station has a city subcentre. The lines of the city hall, which remind one of Notre Dame, jostle with hotels and other skyscrapers.

Harajuku and Aoyama

The name 'Harajuku' covers the entire area from Harajuku station to the east portion of Meiji Dori Street and the areas around the avenue, Omotesando. Originally Omotesando served as a street for pilgrims going to the Meiji shrine. After the Second World War, officers of the GHQ (General Headquarters) spent their days off here and the area took on an atmosphere heavily influenced by Western culture. In a word Harajuku is eclectic. Harajuku has a daytime culture with an up-market Champs Élysées feel while other parts have a lot in common with the more unconventional shops and clubs of London's Soho or New York's East Village. The difference would be that Harajuku has little nightlife, with the people who come shopping here during the day going to Shinjuku, Shibuya and Roppongi at night. Harajuku divides into two main sections along Omotesando and Takeshita Street that run parallel to one another.

Wealthy women sporting the latest in *haute couture* saunter along the international-feeling Omotesando, which offers a pot-pourri of dressy and casual boutiques. Omotesando climaxes with the staked-out territory of LVMH's crown brands. On the other hand, goths, club kids and punks loiter around the nearby Takeshita Street and Yoyogi Park. Takeshita Street targets people in their teens and early 20s with its casual fashions, cheap-chic outlets and 100-yen shops. The roads and the tree-lined pavements are spacious, and fashion-related companies, stores and offices congregate in the area. The shops of famous brands line both sides of the avenue and one can walk the streets much more easily than in either Shinjuku or Shibuya. Since the 1990s, fashionistas might well find combing these backstreets a more fruitful source of exciting and stylish discoveries than the high-profile outlets on the main thoroughfares.

Dubbed with the moniker 'Urahara', the 'backstreets of Harajuku' applies specifically to the 400–500 metre radius around where Meiji Dori intersects with the bazaar-like Takeshita Street. This word derives from the word '*ura*' which means 'back, underground, counter and the other side' combined with the '*hara*' from the name 'Harajuku'. Dozens of independent brands choose to do business here. In this case 'backstreet' certainly does not equate with 'cheap' as many stores sell expensive merchandise.

Aoyama & Omotesandoh Map

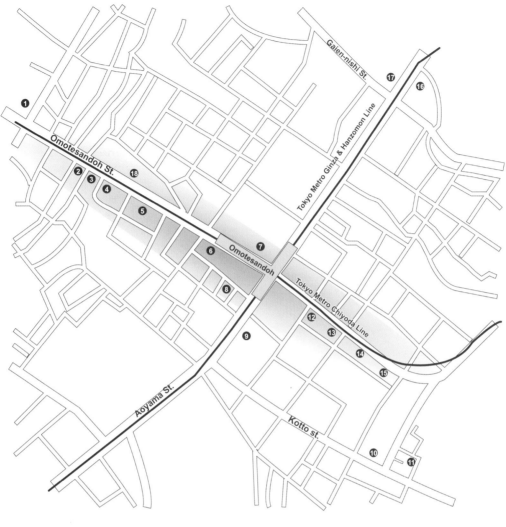

1 LAFORET HARAJUKU
2 CHANEL
3 Christian Dior
4 TAG Heuer
5 LOUIS VUITTON
6 HANAE MORI Bdg
7 ONE
8 GUCCI
9 SPIRAL
10 MARNI
11 MARS THE PLACE
12 COMME des GARCONS
13 PRADA
14 YOJI YAMAMOTO
15 ISSEY MIYAKE FETE
16 Baisouin
17 WATARI-UM
18 DOJUNKAI

A good number of the stores' owners also design the interiors of these shops. Until recently the Doujunkai Apartments stood near Harajuku on Omotesando. This housing complex, which could almost have been called the symbolic landmark of Harajuku, has been torn down to make way for the Tadao Ando-designed Doujunkai Building that is presently under construction.

After going past Aoyama Dori Street (Route 246) and moving away from Harajuku station one enters Aoyama where even more expensive brand stores than in Omotesando line the streets. Here are Future Systems' Comme des Garçons as well as Herzog & de Meuron's Prada.

Shibuya

The department stores Tokyu and Seibu shaped Shibuya into the area it is today. People consider it the dispersal place for fashion, but the profile of Shibuya has faded in recent years. Seibu, a department-store chain based in Ikebukuro, brought its business to Shibuya in 1968

1 United Bamboo
2 CHRISTIAN LACROIX
3 HILLSIDE TERRACE
4 DAZZLING
5 Hoyahoya
6 COCUE
7 YEBISU GARDEN PLACE

providing the impetus for the district to become a cultural centre. In 1973, on a slope now known as Koen Dori, Seibu erected the Parco building; with its fashion industry tenants it drew crowds of fashion-conscious young people attracted by the innovative graphic designs and superior merchandising. The owners put energy into cultural events and the area quickly went from lacklustre to trend central.

Not to be outdone by Seibu, in 1978 Tokyu opened Tokyu Hands, which brought together a unique selection of diverse shops, and then followed this up with the fashion tenant building 'Tokyu 109' which stands out at a

prominent intersection. The icing on the cake came in 1989 when Tokyu created Bunkamura, a cultural complex that combines a gallery, concert hall and theatre. In the 1980s and 1990s teenagers led the way in creating youth culture in Shibuya. Tokyu 109 basked in the limelight in the 1990s when female sales assistants called 'power salespeople' made their debut. The media focused on sales assistants who could rack up 100 million yen worth of clothing sales in one month in a store only 82.6 metres square. From the end of the 1980s, since reliance on the purchasing power of the young meant low returns, the businesses that were based in Shibuya adopted a strategy of attracting adult customers. These strategies included Tokyu's move to open a hotel, shopping and office complex called Mark City which connects directly with the station. Since then Seibu's umbrella organisation, the Saison Group, has succumbed to the inevitable results of mismanagement and, along with its decline, Shibuya as an area has gradually lost some of its individuality and is becoming more and more like Shinjuku.

Daikanyama, Nakameguro and Ebisu

As these three areas lie within easy reach of Shibuya their development might be considered an extension of Shibuya's influence. Daikanyama lies one station away on the Tokyu train. If one arrives with high expectations, one might well feel let down on coming out of the station to be met with such relatively nondescript surroundings. However, just down the road along Yamate Dori on a hillside terrace sits the much-lauded architecture and city block layout designed by Fumihiko Maki. Centred on this area, fashion retail stores line the narrow streets and cater to a crowd that demands the very latest fashions.

Nakameguro is one station down the Tokyu Line from Daikanyama. Some of Daikanyama's prestige has rubbed off on this area and gradually many fashionable stores have sprouted up with many from the fashion industry taking a fancy to the place. This area consistently scores high in the rankings of places where young people would most like to live. Redevelopment is now under way, including a high-rise building in front of the station.

People know Ebisu as the home of the leisure centre complex, Ebisu Garden Place. Situated adjacent to Shibuya, one can walk to Ebisu from Daikanyama in 15 minutes. The location of this area is important because it is near both Shibuya and Daikanyama, and people in the bar and restaurant business and fashion industries pay particular attention to Ebisu. The commercial complex Conze Ebisu is presently under construction near the station.

Roppongi and Nishi Azabu

Roppongi has recently garnered attention due to the opening of Roppongi Hills, a large-scale development that has become a new sightseeing spot. After the Second World War, this district had the distinction of being an area frequented by those involved with the American occupational forces, and was originally geared to adult entertainment with many jazz clubs. Today, jazz clubs have decreased with discos and nightclubs filling their shoes. Roppongi is popular with foreigners, and when night falls a drink-fuelled party atmosphere prevails. Kisho Kurokawa's National Art Exhibition Centre is scheduled to open here in 2006.

Azabu borders Roppongi and has a shopping arcade that has a nostalgic air and gives glimpses of the old downtown of Edo. Developers have set their sights on making Azabu a classy residential area. There are a number of high-rises, such as Shozo Uchii's Moto-Azabu Hills, a rather imposing 29-storey building shaped like a Guinness glass. Nishi Azabu is situated between Omotesando and Roppongi and has many clubs, restaurants and bars that attract the young.

Ginza, Shiodome, Marunouchi and Nihonbashi

These four areas abutt one another. The name Ginza comes from the fact that the minting foundry (*za*) for silver (*gin*) currency operated in this vicinity. In 1872 a fire almost completely destroyed the whole area, and the government commissioned Thomas James Walters from England to lay out the district's design, whereupon Walters planned it in the style of a Georgian town. Subsequently, the Great Kanto Earthquake of 1923 caused considerable damage while four bombing raids in 1945 obliterated almost everything, and after the war redevelopment was begun from scratch. The residents of the area clung to their pride and stayed, intent on creating a world-class commercial district. They still boasted the highest tenant rates in Tokyo. Then prestigious and well-respected stores lined the streets and even today many domestic and international luxury brands have outlets here.

In 1872, a train line was constructed that connected Tokyo and Yokohama with a line coming out of Shinbashi, and created a 31-hectare terminal cargo station at Shiodome. This station was torn down in 1986 and the commercial and cultural facility Caretta Shiodome was erected on the site in 2002. On the west side of Shiodome station, developers are constructing a 5.5-hectare facility fusing housing, office and commercial areas, and copying the style of an Italian streetscape. To be called Città Italia, this project aims for completion in 2007. People call the area nestled between Shiodome and Shinbashi 'Shiosite', and it is densely packed with large corporate office buildings.

Marunouchi lies near Ginza to the front of Tokyo station and might be called the face of Tokyo business. Symbolic of this area, the Maru Building (erected in 1923) underwent renovation in 2002. At 37 storeys many of the stores it accommodates rent space as tenants. As one of Tokyo's new sightseeing attractions, the design here is second to none and the building has the highest posted land value in Japan with its 2004 rates going for 18.7 million yen per square metre. Stimulated by this development, the 20-storey Coredo Nihonbashi was built with a similar concept to the Maru Building. Kohn Pederson Fox Associates were responsible for this building's construction in Ginza's neighbouring Nihonbashi area, and it opened in 2004. The Coredo Nihonbashi might be interpreted as emerging from the friction between the Maru Building's Mitsubishi-associated developer and Coredo's rival Mitsui-associated developer.

Commercial listings

EAT

Soho's Omotesando
Jingumae 6-31-17, Shibuya-ku,
Phone: +81 3 5468 0411

Hoya Hoya
Ebisu-nishi 1-8-3, Shibuya-ku,
Phone; +81 3 5459 4546

Renma Shibuya
Udagawa-cho 24-2, Shibuya-ku,
Phone: +81 3 5459 7851

Oto Oto
http://www.ramla.net/
Ebisu 4-20-4, Shibuya-ku,
Phone: +81 3 5791 7666

Shinobutei Izumi
http://www.med-dining.jp/
Jinnan 1-19-14, Shibuya-ku,
Phone: +81 3 3780 6648

Seiryumon Ueno
http://www.soho-s.co.jp/
Ueno 4-4-5, Taito-ku,
Phone: +81 3 5807 2111

J-Pop Cafe Odaiba
http://www.j-popcafe.com/
Diaba 1-6-1, Minato-ku,
Phone: +81 3 5570 5767.

SHOP

APC Underground
http://www.apc.fr/
Jingumae 4-27-6, Shibuya-ku,
Phone: +81 3 5775 7216

Y's Roppongi Hills
http://www.yohjiyamamoto.co.jp/
Roppongi 6-12-4, Minato-ku,
Phone: +81 3 5413 3434

Louis Vuitton Roppongi Hills
http://www.vuitton.com/
Roppongi 6-12-3, Minato-ku,
Phone: +81 3 3478 2100

Miss Sixty Meijidori
http://www.misssixty.com/
Jingumae 6-25-14, Shibuya-ku,
Phone: +81 3 5464 1428

Q ❤ Flagship Ebisu-nishi
Ebisu-nishi 1-30-10, Shibuya-ku,
Phone: +81 3 5456 9117

United Bamboo
http://www.unitedbamboo.com/
Sarugaku-cho 20-14, Shibuya-ku,
Phone: +81 3 6415 7766

WORK

Beacon Communications Office
JR Tokyu Meguro Bldg.
Kami-Osaki 3-1-1
Shinagawa-ku

Shu Uemura Atelier
Aoyama

Trans Building Office and Gallery
http://www.trans-g.com/
Ebisu-minami 2-12-19, Shibuya-ku,
Phone: +81 3 5720 6472

Ogilvy & Mather Japan
Yebisu Garden Place Tower 25F
Ebisu 4-20-3
Shibuya-ku

Sony Showroom & Qualia Tokyo
http://www.sonybuilding.jp/sr/
Ginza 5-3-1, Chuo-ku,
Phone: +81 3 3573 2563

RELAX

Baisouin Temple
http://baisouin.or.jp/
Minami-aoyama 2-26-38, Minato-ku

Lounge NEO
http://www.clubasia.co.jp/
Dogenzaka 2-21-7, Shibuya-ku,
Phone: +81 3 5428 5739

FIORIA aria blu, Tokyo
http://www.fioria.co.jp/
Roppongi 5-1-3, Minato-ku,
Phone: +81 3 5413 8877

Avalon
Dogenzaka 1-17-9
Shibuya-ku

Mars the Salon
http://www.mars-salon.com/
Minami-aoyama 6-4-6, Minato-ku,
Phone +81 3 5455 8860

Bibliography

Roland Barthes, *L'Empire des Signes.* English translation *The Empire of Signs* (Farrar, Straus & Giroux, 1983). Intellectual city theory inspired by the renowned French critic's experience in Tokyo.

Philippe Pons, *D'Edo a Tokyo* (From Edo to Tokyo) Gaillimard, 1988; Chikumashobo, 1992 (Japanese translation). Insightful literature on Tokyo from historical, sociological, and philosophical viewpoints. English translation unavailable.

Peter Popham, *Tokyo: The City At The End of The World* (Kodansha International, 1985). Must-have book on modern architecture and city development in Tokyo.

Edward G Seidensticker, *Tokyo Rising: The City Since the Great Earthquake* (Knopf, 1990). Full of interesting stories and historical facts.

Deyan Sudjic, *Hundred Mile City* (Harvest Books, 1993). Covers parts of Tokyo intriguingly.

Michio Chimura, *Sengo Fashion Story* (A Story of the Post-war Fashion) Heibonsha, 1989. A concise history of Japanese fashion design after the second world war. Japanese text only.

Masaaki Takahashi, 'Dining Retreat in Tokyo' in *Food and Architecture*, *Architectural Design*, guest-edited by Karen Franck (Wiley-Academy, 2002). Illustrates and discusses recent trends in restaurant design.

Masaaki Takahashi, 'A Housing Boom Embraces High Design' in *Property Development + Progressive Architecture*: *The New Alliance*, *Architectural Design* guest-edited by David Sokol. (Wiley-Academy, 2004, vol. 74, no1). Discusses design and housing in Japan.

GA Japan, no.60, 2003 (pp106–116). An article on Baisoin Temple by Kengo Kuma.

I'm home no13, winter 2003 (pp149–54). An article on K House by Shinichi Ogawa.

Jyutakubunka, December 2001 (pp 34–7), An article on SAK by Toshiaki Ishada.

Jyutakubunka December 2001 (pp 86–89). An article on Natural Illuminance by Masaki Endo.

Shinkenchiku, July 2002 (pp108–114). An article on Plastic House by Kengo Kuma.

Shotenkenchiku, October 2002 (pp111–14). An article on A.P.C. Underground by Laurent Deroo.

Shotenkenchiku, August 2003 (pp118–23). An article on SONY Showroom & Qualia Tokyo by Gwenael Nicholas.

Shotenkenchiku, October 2003 (pp 98–102). An article on Miss Sixty Meijidori by Studio 63.

Shotenkenchiku, February 2004 (pp 90–96). An article on Y's Roppongi Hills by Ron Arad.

Much of the project information in this book is based upon interviews with the architects and interior designers, and data from Japanese websites.